"Daddy, where's your vagina?"

"Daddy, where's your vagina?"

*What I learned as
a stay-at-home dad*

Joseph Schatz

Library of Congress Control Number: 2009910116
ISBN: Hardcover   978-1-4415-8396-3
               Softcover   978-1-4415-8395-6

To order additional copies of this book, contact:
Xlibris Corporation
1-888-795-4274
www.Xlibris.com
Orders@Xlibris.com
66993

CONTENTS

Section 1
Reading between the Lines

Section 2
Dad 2.0

Section 3
The Experienced Parent

Acknowledgments

Writing this book has been an up and down journey for me. Because I am a stay-at-home dad with a fragile ego, I needed the encouragement and assistance from a team of people—thankfully, that's exactly what happened. First, I would like to thank my Dad for being an inspiration to me as a boy and as an adult. My Dad has always been there to show me the lighter side of life and the value of humility. Without his influence this book would not even be a possibility. Next, I would like to thank my good friend Deb Zavoyna. Deb, a fellow full-time parent, was the first person to encourage me to write about my stay-at-home dad experiences and for that I will always be grateful. Like Deb, my Aunt Kathy Williams encouraged me to write, Kathy inspired me to take my blog and turn it into a book—thank you Kathy for believing in me enough to push me to write a book, your faith in me means so much. I would like to thank my editor Beth Bruno for the guidance and patience that she showed me as a first-time author. A special shout out to my brother-in-law and fellow stay-at-home dad Jason Williams. A talented photographer, Jason took the picture that you see as the cover. More than that Jason has always been a good friend and was always there for me to lean on for advice and insight during the writing of my book. Finally, I would like to thank my wife and family. Thank you to my three beautiful daughters, Isabella, Madeleine and Sophia. Girls, you may not know this, but I have learned more from you being your dad than I could ever hope to teach you. It has been the greatest privilege of my life being your father and I am so thankful for my time home with you. Thanks for putting up with me during the summer I wrote this book. I spent a lot of time writing—even during our vacation. You have been so very patient and for that I am eternally grateful. Lastly, I would like to thank my wife, Jodi. Jodi, you are my hero and best friend. Thank you for helping me along my journey through this book but also during my time as a stay-at-home dad. Thanks for taking the girls to the beach by yourself each morning during our trip to Cape May. Thanks for giving me free time on the weekends to write without distraction. Thanks for being a constant source of inspiration to me as a husband, father and writer. I love you. Enough mushy crap—on to the book!

Intro

10:14 AM, October 17, 2006, Churchville, Maryland—Churchville Recreation Center

I was sitting in the lobby feeding Sophia and minding my own business. Sophia was in her car seat, guzzling away on a bottle. We were waiting for her big sister, Mady, to finish up a tumbling class. Like any other day at the rec center, I listened to all the moms talk among themselves. In the month since the class started, many of the moms had become good friends. I remained an outsider.

I didn't take my girls to activities to meet other parents or talk to adults, but it sure would be nice if every once in a while I did get a chance to talk to someone.

That's when it happened. A mom came up to me to talk. It was completely nerdy, but I was kind of excited about the prospect. A mom sitting on the bench about ten feet from mine had just finished talking to another woman; she turned in my direction, and we made eye contact. I smiled at her.

"Excuse me," she started, "I couldn't help but notice *you* are the one that brings your daughter to class each week and *not* your wife."

"Yeah, that's right," I replied in a friendly tone. *Where could this possibly be going?* I wondered.

"So are you a stay-at-home dad?" she asked.

"Yep. I am." I started to feel like a curiosity. "Why do you want to know, if you don't mind my asking?"

"Well, I wanted to know if you were one of those stay-at-home dads that just watches the kids, or do you do the laundry and dishes and stuff?" she asked skeptically.

Huh? Seriously, was this what I had been waiting for? The inquisition. A little stunned, I answered, "Yeah, I do the laundry, the dishes, and I also take out the trash, shovel the snow, and mow the lawn." *This is unbelievable*, I thought. Here's a woman I've never met, and she's asking me if I do the laundry.

"Oh, OK. I was just curious how it worked in your family," she said as if she were saying good-bye forever. She was very direct with me almost as if she were talking to someone not worth her time. I was offended by her question, but I was sure she never thought twice about it. Ninety percent of the time, I would die for another adult to talk to; and 90 percent of the time, I was ignored. When the opportunity finally came along, the person asked if I do the dishes. Nice.

I exchanged smiles with the woman on a few occasions after that, but we never spoke again. Being a stay-at-home dad is a lot like that. We are often a misunderstood breed. A lot of people don't know what to make of us, but we're really no different than any other parent.

Seriously, when our babies are full, do they not poop? Do we not suffer sleep deprivation? Do we not carry diaper bags? Push strollers? Smell like formula? Why is it so hard to figure us out?

In my nine years as a stay-at-home dad, friends, family, and strangers have called me *babysitter, slacker,* and *gay.* Stay-at-home moms have both shunned and celebrated me. I have been the envy of other dads and the butt of their jokes. At times, my fight for respect has seemed to be never ending. There were even dissenters in the ranks of my own family who told me it was wrong for a dad to stay home and raise a family. Raising a family was *women's work.*

Raising my daughters has taught me a lot. It has taught me that guys connect their egos too much to their careers. It has taught me that there is no such thing as *women's work* and that raising kids can be one of the toughest jobs out there especially when you have no road map.

My wife, Jodi, gave me a road map to fatherhood once. It was my first Father's Day as a stay-at-home dad, and fittingly, she bought me a *dad book.* I remember I had one of those honey-what's-this looks on my face when I got it. There was a big-ass penguin on the cover. I was confused. Quickly, she told me that book was about dad emperor penguins and how they cared for their kids, kind of like how I did—minus the whole sitting on a nest in the Antarctic making squawky-bird-noises thing of course. It was the thought that counted. She could tell that I would have preferred a book geared toward my own species.

Let me say that if you aren't a *human* dad—*Daddy, where's your vagina? might not be for you.* Also, how did you even read up to this point in the first place?

What can you expect to get out of this book? Humor. Tips. Insight. This book is the road map I needed when my wife and I decided that I was going to trade in my work boots and hard hat for a baby bottle and diaper bag. It is a mix of my stay-at-home-dad stories and introspection, and tricks of the parenting trade from the perspective of the average guy just trying to get it right. It's a journey from diapers and babies to preschoolers and minivans. I wrote this book with stay-at-home dads in mind, but I think there is a lot moms can learn from this book too. I even promise to go light on the penguins.

Section 1
Reading between the Lines

When I was growing up, I remember aunts, uncles, grandparents —and of course—my mom and dad asking me, "What do you want to be when you grow up?" I'm pretty sure that I never once said, "I want to be a stay-at-home dad." And I'm positive I never said, "I want to wipe butts. Dirty little baby butts—oh, and I would also like to be covered in vomit occasionally for good measure,"—but that's exactly what happened.

A little background is in order. I met my wife, Jodi, when we were sixteen. Yeah, I know, my name is Joe and my wife's name is Jodi—fate, right? I trained her to scoop ice cream at a Friendly's Restaurant. She, almost immediately, fell head over heels in love with me.

After some aggressive maneuvering on her part, namely, her kissing me, I got the point; and we became an item. We became best friends almost instantly, and although that alienated us from our existing group of hormonally challenged acquaintances, we never looked back. We married at the young age of twenty-one (me) and twenty (her).

Jodi and I worked our way from apartment to apartment and, eventually, to a town house in Towson, Maryland. We had gone from waiting tables in college to my job as a construction supervisor and hers as a technical assistant for an engineering firm. We had taken a break from full-time school with a serious case of identity crisis. We *thought* we wanted to be teachers, but the student teaching convinced us to reconsider. We did know that we loved each other more than enough to start a family.

We tried. For months we tried. Nothing happened. *Were we doing it right?* I thought we were. After scratching seven months of failure up to *poor aim,* we came to the realization that something wasn't right. Why couldn't we conceive?

Doctors pointed their instruments immediately at Jodi. I found it odd that it was assumed Jodi had something wrong with her. *Why not me?* Not that I wanted doctors poking around down there or anything. After a few tests, it was determined Jodi had *endometriosis.*

I was relieved. My penis was in working order, and it didn't have to be tested. I did feel bad for Jodi though—she hated seeing doctors.

Up to this point in her life, Jodi had always been a needle-fearing, hospital—and doctor-hating maniac. However, once she knew what had to be done in order to have children, she turned into a callous model of strength. She never bragged about overcoming her fear; she just kind of did it—overnight. She marched through blood tests and examinations, leading up to and including surgery. The procedure only took an hour or so. I remember our doctor coming out into the waiting room in the hospital where I sat with Jodi's mom and dad.

"It was a success. Jodi is recovering now, and you will be able to visit her soon," the doctor told us.

"That's great! Thank you so much, Doc," I said as I shook his hand. As I stood there, I had the realization that I was going to be a dad soon. I was ecstatic. "So how long should we wait before we start trying again?" I asked eagerly.

"You can start trying in a month."

"Really? That soon?" I was surprised. My wife just had surgery. It seemed too quick.

With a laugh, he replied, "Yes, a month is the generally recommended recovery time."

"OK, thanks again!"

We were pregnant the following month.

As all the drama played out behind the scenes, my wife had moved up into configuration management and had her eye on a software-testing job. My career was different. I worked long, hard hours. I had no benefits. My boss handled his money poorly. Although I made more money, there were times when I was told I couldn't cash my paycheck. It was easy to see who had the more promising career.

When the reality set in that a baby was on the way, we started crunching the numbers. *What were we going to do once the baby was born?* It didn't take a rocket scientist to see that pound for pound Jodi's job offered more mobility and benefits and was less abusive physically.

We really couldn't think of a reason for me to stay in my job unless my boss—a close friend of mine—would concede benefits to me.

"Joe, I just can't do it" was the predictable answer he gave me when I asked for a health care plan. I understood that he was limited as a small-business owner in what he could do for his employees. So there it was, my wife was going to work full-time, and I was going to be home with the baby.

There is a certain fear that accompanies a decision that leads you down a road untraveled. I was afraid of being a stay-at-home dad. I was afraid of what people would think of me. *Would they think I was some kind of slacker, loser, moocher? What would our neighbors think? Our friends? Our family? I was afraid I couldn't do the job. What did I know about babies? How hard would changing a diaper be? Could I handle a sick baby? A crying baby? Anything?*

The Difference between Boys and Girls

Not only do girls expect to be moms someday, but they also start their training very early on. Girls grow up playing house, playing with baby dolls, pushing toy strollers, and flipping plastic pancakes with plastic spatulas in their plastic kitchens. I had GI Joes and Transformers. If you dug through my toy chest, you might think I would have a career in freedom fighting or advanced robotics—not fatherhood.

My college prep high school taught me everything I needed to know about the Magna Carta but nothing about changing diapers. In college, I learned my way through education psychology and Matthew Arnold, but no one showed me how to use a nasal aspirator—let alone tell me what one was.

I don't think our neighborhood helped ease my concerns about being a stay-at-home dad either. The neighborhood we lived in was chock-full of stay-at-home moms. The first year or so after we moved in, we felt like outsiders. We went to a few parties and mingled, but we kept getting the feeling that we just weren't part of the *in crowd*.

First, we were younger—like ten years younger than everyone else. Besides that, we didn't have kids. We couldn't figure out if it was our age or the lack of progeny that made us feel like outcasts. One night at a neighborhood get-together, a woman in her midthirties told us in the nicest way possible that we really needed to have a kid to *fit in*. That was the tone of our neighborhood.

When the neighborhood ladies found out we were pregnant, it was like we had a second welcome-to-the-neighborhood party. We were finally *legit*.

The moms in the neighborhood had a million and one questions for Jodi. *How did she feel? How far along was she? Did we have any names picked out? What was the due date? Was she excited to be a mom—a full-time mom?* The moms were none too pleased to find out that I would be the one at home—they were looking forward to getting to know Jodi. Conversations with the moms in the area usually went something like this:

A neighborhood mom exclaimed, "I am so excited for you guys!"

Jodi said, "Thank you. We're really excited too!"

The neighborhood mom continued, "You're going to love being a mom, and the neighborhood has so many young kids—you'll fit right in."

"I know. Everywhere we turn, we see young families. We had no idea the neighborhood would be like this when we moved in. It really seems like a great place to raise a family," Jodi answered.

"Well, after you have the baby, you are going to have to join the 'Bagel Club.' All the stay-at-home moms in the neighborhood take turns hosting. It's a lot of fun," the neighborhood lady said.

"Actually, I am going to be the one staying home," I interjected.

A short awkward silence followed. Finally, the neighborhood lady replied, "Oh, well, you're more than welcome to hang out too!" Somehow, the invitation sounded disingenuous.

"Great! I look forward to it." Almost immediately, I knew I had a label on me. I could tell moms already regarded me as substandard or some kind of second-rate replacement for the *real thing*.

I think someone explained what the "Bagel Club" was to me like five times before I really got the concept. Basically, it was just women getting together to talk, drink coffee, and let their kids interact with the other neighborhood kids. It felt awkward just picturing myself sitting among the throngs of coffee-drinking women. I knew I had to take care of the baby and handle most of the cooking and cleaning, but *mingling*? I could already see this new subculture was going to give me fits.

Watching my wife's first pregnancy progress, I couldn't help but measure my anxiety by Jodi's ever-inflating waistline. Every day I had a physical reminder that the clock was ticking. I was going to be on my own. At home. With a baby.

Jodi had horrible morning sickness and woke up vomiting every morning for eight months. This was new territory for both of us as my wife, a normally calculated logical sort of woman, started to battle emotional highs and lows. Jodi was poked and prodded by doctors, administered tests, and in and out of hospital gowns for a total of six sonograms. She seemed numb to all the invasiveness that she once dreaded in the past. The pregnancy had changed her; it had given her thick skin.

After the sixth sonogram, the doctor proclaimed that we were having a girl. We chose the name Isabella, got our bags packed, and waited for the day to arrive. Then it happened. Just when I thought I couldn't be more impressed with my wife, she went into labor.

It started with the "bloody show." Now, for all of you guys out there who are expecting your first child or thinking about starting a family, I need to tell you something candidly—labor and delivery are no picnic. All your training tells you to breathe and remain calm, but it's really difficult to be *calm* when you are minutes away from a life-changing experience.

During Bella's delivery, the doctor told us that there were *complications*. Jodi needed to have an emergency *C-section*. Apparently, Bella's umbilical cord was wrapped around her neck, and she was losing oxygen each time there was a contraction. So the doctor prepped my wife, and the nurses threw me in scrubs. We were in the OR in about five minutes.

Jodi had a flawless *C-section*. It was quick too. In what seemed like only a few minutes, we became parents. It was the single most moving experience of our lives. Isabella was perfect and beautiful. After three and a half days in the hospital, Jodi and I returned home and began our adventures in parenting.

The fact that Jodi had a *C-section* meant I was the one changing all the diapers. I was the one taking care of all the initial rocking and burping. It was good training, and it gave me a lot of confidence. I learned so much about taking care of a baby during those initial first few weeks. Jodi was in a considerable amount of pain for around a month. So not only was I taking care of Bella, but I also had to look in on Jodi too.

I was amazed at how easily I took to this whole *baby thing*. *If it were just the three of us, life would be so easy,* I thought. We were so perfect together, but Jodi had to return to work, and I had to start my career at home with Bella.

The Problem with Male Pride

I have to say, our immediate family was very supportive of our choices. I don't know if I expected some sort of public outrage because I was home full-time, but it never happened. The reality was that the person who had the most trouble adjusting to me staying home was *me*.

Whenever I talked to someone and they asked me what I did for a living, I found myself saying in an apologetic voice, "I stay home with my daughter." It was as if I was waiting for someone to chastise me for being different. I think *male pride* can be a tough pill to swallow.

I know it's weird, but I had a tough time filling out the routine forms at doctor's offices. I would get to the part where they asked for my work address or work phone number, and I would stop. *Why are they asking me this? Don't they know I don't have a job? Are they just trying to rub it in?* Typically, I would hunch over and fill out those parts in secret and return the form when no one was looking.

Why was it hard for me to admit what I was—an awesome dad?

Bella and I were very active. We ran errands together. We went to the grocery store and to doctor appointments. We would go to a park about fifteen minutes up the road and do some fishing and throw rocks in the water. I rode her around on my bike, and we went for walks around the neighborhood. With each stop at the store and trip to the doctors, I was becoming more confident and empowered as a dad. I felt like we were ready for the Bagel Club.

I had a mental image of what the Bagel Club would be like. I pictured parents playing with kids, kids playing with other kids, and parents talking to other parents. I was wrong. It turned out that the Bagel Club was a forum for the neighborhood moms to gripe about their husbands, gossip, and inevitably talk about their pregnancies.

We went to the Bagel Club regularly. I kept giving it another chance. I felt like maybe the neighborhood moms would warm up to me; instead, I often found myself a bystander in women-centric conversations. The moms talked about celebrity interviews on *Oprah* or about who was the hottest guy in our neighborhood. Sometimes the moms would talk about their sagging boobs or about how fat they were getting. It was awkward and uncomfortable at the Bagel Club, but I continued to go for Bella. I really enjoyed seeing her play with other little kids. I was happy at least one of us was having some success socially.

Those first nine months were probably the toughest on me. My battle with my self-image hit an all-time low that first Christmas. I remember one of the toughest concepts I had to overcome was the act of Christmas shopping for my wife with *her* money. Sure, the money she makes is *our* money, but my ego had a tough time wrestling with the notion that I could buy her something with *our* money and say it was from *me.*

My first Christmas home I went way overboard on Jodi. I bought her everything. I felt guilty that I was home taking care of Bella. I felt guilty that I couldn't buy her something with money that *I* had earned. I felt inferior in a lot of ways. She had seventeen boxes to open, and each one was a testament to my crumbling self-esteem.

Yes, it took me awhile to overcome my ego. Yes, it took me awhile to grab some esteem from being a stay-at-home dad. I think it's harder for dads to recognize and accept that child care is a productive and helpful contribution to the family. The turning point for me was when family members, friends, and strangers started noticing and complimenting Bella. I was doing something right as a dad.

Don't fall into that same trap. Recognize that you aren't any less of a man for making the tough choice to raise your family. Take pride in your role. Embrace your position in life.

Getting Respect

For her part, Bella was remarkably smart, easy to take care of, and lovable. Bella walked at nine months and began talking around the same time. Her first words were "thank you," pronounced as "da-doo." Before long, Bella was speaking in sentences, identifying colors and shapes, and off the charts in cuteness.

When Bella was around a year and a half, I started working a part-time job at a local wine superstore as a salesman. The years I spent working in restaurants meant I was pretty knowledgeable when it came to wine. The store was only a two-minute drive up the road, and the work was more than tolerable. I thrived in the laid-back atmosphere of retail. The people and product appealed to me, and although I only worked twenty hours a week, it was great therapy.

Also, around this time, we found out we were pregnant with number two. Our family was growing, and Bella was going to be a big sister. From as early as we could, we pushed the *big sister* angle with Bella. The last thing we wanted her to think was that a new baby would steal any of her thunder. We impressed the fact on her that we would need her help with the baby and that the new baby was excited to see her.

Just after Bella's second birthday, I started my own *daddy day care*. My day care operation started when a single father in the neighborhood asked me if I would watch his four-year-old boy a few days a week. The father, Steve, knew me from around the neighborhood and a basketball league we played in together. Steve could see that Bella and I were active. His son, Eric, on the other hand, was spending his days idle in the house with his grandmom watching TV. Steve asked if I would be interested in watching his son a couple days a week with the hopes of getting him out of the house.

I accepted. We never turned down money, and I thought it would be good for both Bella and me having another kid around during the day. Eric already knew how to ride a bike, and he loved getting out of the house, so it was a good fit. We did breakfast and lunch together, and I worked with him occasionally on some preschool books as he prepared for kindergarten.

That summer, watching Eric was great. I learned a lot taking care of two kids at the same time. It really helped me prepare for the juggling act of handling two of my own kids. More than that, it was cool that I was respected enough as a parent to be given the chance to watch someone else's child. *Respect is a very cool thing as a parent.*

Just as I stopped watching Eric, Mady entered the picture. The delivery went over without complication. She was healthy but small.

Adjusting to the Second Child

Jodi had some mending to do after the delivery, so I was pretty much a full-time father to two girls from the moment Mady was born. Naturally, I was in charge of diaper changes, getting them dressed and fed, and making sure Bella wasn't crowding the new baby too much during their first few days together.

Bella stayed in our hospital room with us in her port-a-crib. So not only was I changing Mady's diapers, but I was also changing Bella's as well. At this point in my stay-at-home career, I considered myself a *diaper pro*. This fact wasn't lost on the nurses either as they marveled at how I changed our newborn's diapers. I was impressive. Imagine that. It was kind of cool being appreciated for something I considered so routine.

Jodi wasn't able to help with the girls until a week after delivery and wasn't at 100 percent until about a month after Mady was born. Once again, the time home when Jodi was on maternity leave was amazing. I absolutely loved being together as a family, and I really missed Jodi when she had to go back to work.

The biggest adjustment I had to make with Mady was accepting the fact that she was different than Bella. For some reason I thought they were going to be clones but they weren't. Bella loved to snuggle. Mady likes her own space. Isabella has fair skin, dark hair, and freckles. Madeleine, although born with dark hair, quickly turned blonde and has naturally tan skin that bronzes in the summer sun. Bella is more extroverted, and Madeleine is content to sit back and observe. Oddly, under pressure, Mady has no problem performing. Bella gets very nervous. I have had many peaceful car rides with Madeleine where neither of us says a word—Bella, on the other hand, is a chatterbox and dislikes silence. The differences between my girls never cease to amaze me.

A lot of people debate which is more important: nature or nurture. In my opinion, there is no argument—nature. Don't get me wrong, being a good parent is a crucial component to giving our children a moral compass and discipline, but their personalities and idiosyncrasies are hardwired.

Mady's milestones came slower than Bella's, and the comparisons were hard to avoid as a parent. Bella had walked at nine months—Madeleine at thirteen. Bella started talking at nine months—Madeleine at twelve. We found ourselves constantly wondering if Mady was *OK*. You just never think as a parent that your kid is *average*, but that's just how Mady developed.

Life moves quicker when you have kids. Holidays, birthdays, and vacations blend together. Diapers, wipes, and sterilized bottles eat up time faster than anything else I have come across. For us, life was on steroids. Why not try for a third child, right? When Mady was one and a half, we moved from our town house in Towson to a single family home in Havre de Grace—we also found out we were expecting number three.

I think one of the greatest moments of joy in my life, besides when our daughters were born, is hearing my wife say the words, "We're pregnant." I still get choked up thinking about it. I can hear the words. I can see her eyes welling with tears. I can feel myself in an almost-out-of-body state. Those are moments that transcend all the trivial, daily-grind stuff. I am pretty sure I cried each time Jodi told me we were pregnant. I guess I'm kind of a baby that way, but I just can't picture reacting any other way to that type of news.

That winter we found out the sex of the baby—we were having another girl. Three girls! At that point, I would have been more anxious if I found out we were having a little boy. I had only taken care of little girls. There was some comfort in finding out we were having another girl. Everything we owned was girl related from the *hand-me-down* clothes, the toys, crib sheets, bibs, and even sippy cups.

Well, I should say we were pretty sure we were having a girl. The doctor said he wasn't 100 percent sure. So we started preparing the baby's room with generic colors like yellow and pale green. We collected baby clothes and bottles from our storage bins and purchased some unisex outfits just in case we did have a boy.

I kind of wondered if it was some sort of conspiracy. *Would the doctor give parents a vague answer about the baby's sex just to boost sales in unisex baby items? Did they make a percentage off the year's receipts?* I had to focus. I had to get number three's room ready—oh, and take care of our other little girls.

From January until March, I was home full-time with Mady while Bella went to kindergarten. During the seven months leading up to the birth of our third child, I had an opportunity to really get to know Mady. She was very different than Bella, and only when you are around a child one on one do you truly begin to appreciate those differences fully.

Mady was quiet and strong-willed. Mady liked her space, but the more time I spent with her, the more she began to open up. I remember during these few months Mady finally decided to snuggle on the couch and watch kids' shows with me. She was two and a half and seemed to finally be warming up to the world—I loved it.

I was talking to Mady a lot about being a big sister and what that meant. I remember Bella cherishing the responsibility of being a big sister, but Mady was not nearly as emotional as Bella—it was a tougher sell. As the months went by, I was more and more curious to see how she would react to having a baby sister. I was very curious to see how Mady would respond to being in the middle. Would it be tough on her?

Our Blue-Collar Baby

Days go by slowly when you are close to delivery. As a dad, you become hypersensitive to your wife, her breathing and subtle pauses. *Is it time?* I kept asking myself in my head. You start thinking more and more about how the baby's name will sound when you say it, and you start thinking up ways to make the entire process go by faster. A friend said that two things worked for them: eating red meat and sex.

The whole sex-with-a-full-term-woman thing has always seemed a little too familiar for me. It is kind of dirty and awkward, in my mind, to try and act all sexy when your wife is getting kicked and punched by a kid-in-utero. What if the baby kicks *me*? I would totally freak.

So, instead, I purchased some aged, prime-cut New York strips. I made a huge meal complete with the steaks, baked potatoes, béarnaise sauce (Jodi loves that stuff), and asparagus. Jodi predictably stuffed herself. She was ravenous—almost like a monster eating a tiny village. And wouldn't you know it, shortly after the massive meal, the contractions started coming. Not the Braxton Hicks teasers, but the consistent, painful contractions that pointed toward the inevitable.

We gathered up Mady, Bella and our overnight bags and headed for the hospital. Even on the twenty-minute drive to the hospital, the contractions began to speed up and get stronger. Jodi was in *real* pain, something that she wasn't accustomed to during her previous two deliveries.

Although painful, the delivery was otherwise smooth, and on pie day (March 14), Sophia Jolie was born. What I remember most about Sophia when she was born was her stature. She looked a lot more **blue-collar** then our first two girls. She looked muscular. She even had shoulder hair—dark, weird shoulder hair. Aside from all that hair, Sophia was absolutely beautiful. She had big eyes, long eyelashes, and a full head of dark hair. Like our other girls, she was small, weighing only five pounds fifteen ounces.

Right after Sophia was born, I remember getting comments from other dads about the *third child*. Apparently, a lot of parents are stuck in the *two-child* box and can't fathom the jump to a *third child*. "I can't imagine how crazy that is," or simply, "Three kids! Wow!"

To be honest, we never thought the jump from one to two was difficult. I mean, being a parent isn't something that ends. Why is there this big sticker shock over making the jump from one to two kids or from two to three? Once you are in the parenting business, you don't get out—you are a *lifer*. That is the mentality my wife and I have always subconsciously brought to the parenting table. Another kid of course brings additional responsibility, diapers and bottles, but as long as you are committed to being a parent, it doesn't matter how many kids you have—you will always be defined by either "Mom" or "Dad."

Special Days

As a baby, Sophia's disposition was perfect. She loved to be held; she slept through the night in her crib at a month and a half, and after two months, she began to let out full-belly laughs. I remember her first laugh—it was that impressive. There I was changing her, and as I was putting on her new diaper, she started laughing—really hard. I was probably either making peekaboo faces at her or singing, but regardless of what I was doing, I remember her laugh. It was a hearty laugh. It was really quite remarkable. Just a couple months prior, Sophia was swimming in amniotic fluid—now she was in front of me chuckling.

Sophia was a quick study as a baby. She pulled herself up and began cruising (walking while holding on to something) at only seven months. She started to walk independently at eight months and was saying small words at around nine months. There was no getting around it—Sophia was advanced. I remember bragging about Bella and how quickly she developed. That was a rookie mistake. By the time we had Sophia, I realized that no one likes a braggy parent. So I took Sophia's progress in stride.

Her first year went by very quickly. Mady was now in a co-op preschool, and Bella was in four different activities. I had begun my taxi service in earnest. If I wasn't running back and forth to the doctor's office with Sophia, I was running to dance, basketball, soccer, or gymnastics with Bella. It wasn't too long before Jodi and I noticed that we felt a little disconnected as a family unit.

We looked for a solution and came up with our *"special day"* philosophy. Jodi and I decided we would try to spend one day with each of our girls alone. For instance, Mommy would take Mady out. They would go to the movies and pick out a book from the library together.

The next week, Daddy would take Mady fishing and out for a milk shake. Each girl would get a turn having their special day.

I remember many of the special days I have spent with my daughters over the years. Although all of the special days have been memorable, the first one with each of them sticks out the most. With Bella, I remember it was late September, and we decided to go fishing. Bella was five years old at the time. Predictably, she talked the entire ride to the reservoir where we were renting a little boat for the morning. *Daddy, what's a lake? Is a lake bigger than the ocean? Daddy, how many fish are there in the lake? Daddy, do they have big teeth? Daddy, are we going to eat them? Daddy, what's the biggest fish you ever caught? Daddy, I have to go potty.*

That morning, when we left the house, it was unseasonably cold. I thought to myself, *It has to warm up as the sun comes out.* Thirty minutes later, when we arrived at the boat rental office, I realized that it wasn't going to warm up—it was just cold. A bit under dressed, Bella and I were both shivering as we headed out and started fishing at Loch Raven reservoir that day. It usually isn't cold enough to see your breath in September in Maryland. "Daddy, it's really cold." Bella told me around twenty times during the first minute or so of being on the water. I had no choice—I took off my windbreaker and wrapped it around Bella. At least she would be warm. After motoring out to a peaceful, secluded fishing spot, Bella asked to use the bathroom. "Honey, there aren't any bathrooms on the boat, but I can pull over to shore and you can go there."

"In the woods?" Bella asked with a really confused look on her face.

"Yes, sweetie, in the woods."

"Oh, OK," she said, letting me know that would be fine. After parking my boat on the closest thing to a beach in the nearby area, I struggled to transfer Bella from the wobbly aluminum boat to the shore. The woods were dense enough to cause Bella problems, but she managed. Over the course of a two-and-a-half-hour span, Bella had to pee around fifteen times. I fell in the water once, and we never caught a fish. I don't recall ever seeing a fish. Bella also got her line stuck on everything. She cast into trees, got stuck on mystery objects under the water, and hooked me a couple times for good measure. Between fixing Bella's line and taking her to the shore to go potty, I may have cast out five times.

I never said it, but to me, I thought the day was a disaster. What was her take though? After returning the boat and getting back in the car, I asked Bella, "So did you have fun?" I was shocked to hear her answer.

"I loved it, Daddy! When can we do it again?" In my mind, the day went terribly wrong, but in the eyes of a child, it was magical. The entire car ride home, Bella talked about the fishing trip. *You remember when you fell in the water, Daddy? You remember when we saw that bird? You remember when I got my line stuck in that big tree? You remember that all the fish were sleeping? That boat was really fun! I can't wait to tell Mama.* It occurred to me then that it didn't matter what we did on our special days, it was just spending time together that was important.

Mady's first special day was very different. Her day came after Bella's, so I was bit more prepared. Mady was three at the time, and instead of renting a boat or trying to do something extravagant, I took her to a local park and playground. In direct contrast to Bella, Mady was almost perfectly quiet the entire car ride to and from the park. It was refreshing. We played at the playground together and walked around the park until she was tired, and then we stopped by a local ice cream shop and bought milk shakes. We sat outside on a bench, drank our milk shakes, and admired the day. As eventful as Bella's day was, was as about as uneventful as Mady's had been. It was just two people enjoying time together and not needing to talk about it. When Mady got home, I wondered if she was going to say she had a good day together. "So, Mady, how was your day?" Jodi asked her.

"It was the best day ever, Mama!" Mady exclaimed. Two completely different days, but both had the same result. It was the attention that was important to our kids, not what we did. The attention made them feel important—special. The special-day tradition has been invaluable to our family. We continue to learn so much from being around our kids one-on-one, and we know they look forward to having special time with each of us. We started special days when Sophia was a year old, and we have kept up the tradition ever since.

I became active in playgroups in our new neighborhood around the time Sophia turned one. Surprisingly, I met a couple of moms at the co-op preschool where Mady went to school that were *really* cool to talk to. Usually, moms avoid stay-at-home-dad conversations, but these moms were different—more laid-back. Deb Zavoyna and Courtney Tramontana are easily two of the most accepting and genuine friends I have ever had. After talking to each other a few times outside of preschool as we waited for dismissal, we decided to start a playgroup. It was great.

The playgroup conversations weren't the standard *Oprah* and pregnancy babble. I finally had some meaningful adult interaction. We talked about our kids, life, news, and politics. We alternated going to each other's houses, and as the weather warmed and the summer came, we took trips to playgrounds and parks. Life was good. Mady and Sophia were able to see some kids their age on a regular basis, *and* I had a peer group that respected me and included me in their conversations.

The summer not only brought trips to playgrounds and parks, but also big news for our family—we were expecting number four.

A Series of Unfortunate Events

We found out we were pregnant with our fourth child just before my thirty-first birthday. I couldn't have been happier. Jodi had always been cautious and supportive since the first day I became a stay-at-home dad. Before we even started trying to have our fourth, she asked me, "Joe, are you sure you want to do this?"

"I'm sure, Jodi," I reassured her.

"You'll be the one who will be sacrificing," she told me. "You will be the one changing most of the diapers. You are going to be tied down for another five years. Are you sure you are ready for that?"

"Jodi, I am sure. I was sure the second we brought it up," I said with a glimmer in my eye.

"OK. I just want to make sure because I don't want you to have any regrets."

"I won't, sweetheart."

We both wanted another kid. Maybe we wanted another kid because we constantly marvel at how amazing our daughters are. Maybe we felt like our hearts had some room left for another rug rat. Maybe it was because we have always been so in love with one another. No matter the reason, we went down that path to have our fourth. In the beginning of May 2007, Jodi found out she was pregnant.

We were busting. When you find out that you are pregnant, it is advised that you shouldn't tell anyone until you are a couple months along, but it is so tough to keep that a secret. We have always had a tough time waiting. We had no intentions of telling anyone just yet, that was before I knew Jodi was throwing me a surprise party. Jodi threw me a surprise birthday party in the beginning of June.

It was a huge surprise because I wasn't expecting anything big for my thirty-first birthday. I remember walking into the house and seeing a ton of people and then walking back out because I was just so shocked. Jodi had assembled all of our friends and family on a Saturday afternoon. It was over the top. There was a huge spread of food and drinks. There were people everywhere. I couldn't believe everyone wanted to celebrate my birthday. It really floored me. Jodi organized every last detail, and it was perfect.

I remember being in our backyard talking to Jodi with forty or fifty of our closest friends. I turned to Jodi and asked her if we could tell everyone our *big news*.

"Jodi, can we tell them?" I whispered.

"Do you want to?" she asked.

"I think it would be really cool if we did. Anyway, everyone is here. It would make it a lot easier just telling everyone this way."

"OK, let's do it," she said excitedly.

I paused and collected myself. When I had some clarity, I said, "Excuse me, could I have everyone's attention!" Everyone turned and looked my way. "First, I just want to thank you for coming today. I am so happy that you are here to celebrate my birthday." I paused again. "Second, I want to share some exciting news with everyone. We're pregnant!" Everyone cheered and clapped their hands. It was truly awesome. The party continued on into the night. It was a magical day and one I will *always* remember.

The days slipped by quickly after the party in large part due to an upcoming vacation. We were looking forward to a weekend trip at Cape May, New Jersey. We arrived there late on a Friday night, and we planned on coming home Sunday night, which would give us two beach days.

Saturday morning, just before we were about to leave for the beach, Jodi grabbed my attention.

"Joe, come here," she said in a secretive tone.

"What's up?" I asked her.

"Joe, I'm bleeding."

"Huh? What are you talking about? Where?" I was clueless.

"*Down there*," she said with desperation. "I think something's wrong." She was nervous and started to shake. "We need to go home."

"OK. I'll get the girls, and you start throwing your stuff in the suitcase." We packed all of our stuff in record time, and the girls, being perfect angels, sensed the gravity of the situation and never once complained. They knew something was wrong with Mommy and the baby, and that was enough for them.

We raced home and, along the way, called Jodi's ob-gyn. He sent us to the hospital for an examination, and even though there was a lot of spotting, they weren't overly concerned; we were though. Jodi knew something wasn't right, and her doctor told her to rest. He told her there was nothing she could do even if she *was* about to have a miscarriage. We googled it to death and found little comfort in what we read. All the Internet could tell us was that if Jodi was about to have a miscarriage, nothing could stop it from happening. That night, she felt increasingly more ill and finally had to get in the shower to battle nausea and stomach cramps.

Shortly after she got in the shower, I heard her let out a bloodcurdling scream.

"Joe! Get . . . in . . . here . . . please!" she paused succinctly as she said each word. It was eerie to hear. It sounded *very bad*.

Sounds stick with me. I remember all of my grandparents' voices even though they are just memories now. I remember how my cat growing up sounded when he meowed. And I vividly remember what Jodi sounded like when she called for my help that night. It was desperation personified.

I rushed to the bathroom, flung the door open, and made my way to the shower. I knew I was opening a portal into something unpleasant as I tugged at the shower door. I knew there was no going back, and that I wasn't going to like what I saw, but I had no choice.

There was Jodi hunched in the shower in hysterics. She was pointing toward the shower floor, but I had already seen *it*. Jodi had apparently tried to push *it* down the drain, but the drain couldn't handle passing *it*. She was crying. She couldn't handle what she was going through. It was too much for her. Someone needed to step in and help. Quickly, I acted on instinct and grabbed up a hand towel and picked up the indescribable carnage of tissues and blood that lay before me. I disposed of *it* the only way I knew how—in the toilet.

As I carried out the dark deed, I couldn't help but wonder what it was I was flushing. I felt like a killer. My head was spinning. I was sick. I felt like I was going to throw up. But something brought me back from the brink—Jodi's tears. She was in way worse shape. I remember holding her in the shower and trying to comfort her. The entire episode lasted maybe two minutes, but it remains with me and always will.

As the days and weeks passed, our family and friends stopped by or sent cards, flowers, and care packages to console my wife. She received a tremendous amount of support. I was there for her too. She was really hit hard by what happened. I was somewhere neither here nor there. I was along for the ride and kept denying the fact that I was shaken up by it.

I think most people view miscarriages as something that only affects women; I know I did. I didn't let myself grieve or really examine what had happened because everyone rallied around my wife. It wasn't until months had passed that it hit me like a ton of bricks.

Being a stay-at-home dad, I was *really* looking forward to another kid. That's not to say my wife was looking forward to another child any less than I was, but I was already mentally prepared for the changes in my life. I was going to have to deal with the diapers and crying kids for that many more years. My professional life was going to be on hold for that many more years. I had already accepted another five years of being a caregiver. Those feelings lingered with me even months after the miscarriage.

It was about four months after the miscarriage that my wife and I got an opportunity to have a date night. That's when the emotions finally caught up with me. That night, Jodi brought up the night of the miscarriage. She asked, "Have you been thinking about it at all?"

It was such a simple question, but the words hit me in a profound way. *Had I been thinking about that night? Of course I had been thinking about it. I was thinking about it every day since it happened. I was thinking about what I had done. I was thinking about what was lost. I was thinking about what could have been.* I was devastated, but I never admitted it to anyone—even myself.

As I started to answer her, I surprised myself by breaking down. I started crying. Not just a tear here and there, but a hard cry. I had obviously held in my grief for too long. I had denied myself the opportunity to deal with what we had lost.

Jodi and I had a long talk about our future and if we should try for another kid. Jodi didn't want to be pregnant in her thirties, so it was now or never. She was also having a lot of trouble even considering having another baby after the miscarriage. I saw the writing on the wall. We weren't going to have another kid. We were done. Our family was set. Joe, Jodi, Bella, Mady, and Sophia. I know the miscarriage hit me really hard, but deciding not to have another child had its consequences too. I was going to return to work as soon as Sophia was in kindergarten instead of when number four made it to elementary school.

My career as a stay-at-home dad was coming to an end. There was light at the end of the tunnel, and it scared me.

Section 2
Dad 2.0

What is *Dad 2.0*? *Dad 2.0* is today's dad. You will become *Dad 2.0* through raising your kids. *Dad 2.0* does it all. We take our kids to their soccer practices. We tuck our kids in at night and drive them to school in the morning. We tell our kids we love them, and we hug them when they get hurt. We even brush our daughter's hair. There is a distinct paradigm shift in the culture of fatherhood.

Dad 2.0 is cooking in the kitchen, folding laundry, and mopping the floors. Nothing is taboo anymore. On top of all the chores and errands that *Dad 2.0* handles on a daily basis, we are also the traditional dad of the '50s and '60s TV shows. We are there to help our kids with homework and help them through the organized chaos of life.

Like the women's movement of the '60s and '70s, the dads' movement we are seeing now is its rival. Dads today are working less and parenting more. Some dads are home once a week with the kids. Some of us work from home the majority of the time. And then there are the stay-at-home dads. They are leaving their jobs completely to stay home with the kids. Dads have more face time with their kids and more domestic responsibilities than ever before.

Dad 2.0 doesn't settle for being a parent on the sidelines, but there are some common pitfalls to watch out for.

The Barrier of Learned Helplessness

Apparently, there is a psychological condition called *learned helplessness*. It is one of those proverbial snowball situations that feeds on itself as it rolls downhill out of control. It starts innocently enough. A mom insisting to change diapers, feed, and burp the baby is one example. She might be thinking she is doing the father a favor, or maybe, she thinks that she is just better suited to change a diaper full of doo. Whatever reason, it becomes a pattern. The child cries; Momma comes running. The child needs a bottle; Mom races to the rescue. During the first year or so, it is easy to let Mom do the *dirty work.*

Werraaaaahhhh! a dad says as he is playing "airplane" with his son.

"Go easy, hon, OK?" his wife says.

"I got it, sweetheart. Umm, uh-oh," the husband says.

"What is it?" the wife asks in a concerned tone.

"Sweetie, junior has a stinky," he replies.

"Phew! He sure does."

"Should I . . . ?" the husband offers.

"No, don't worry, I got it." She hops up and snatches the baby out of his hands.

Sometimes, the moms are just more assertive. Sometimes the dads feel like they are getting in the way.

"Is this how you do it?" a husband asks his wife who is leaning over his shoulder, watching him change a diaper.

"Well, make sure you clean real good," she says anxiously.

"Like this?" he replies.

"Well . . . no . . . wait . . . let me show you again." She steps in.

What couples like these fail to see is the trap they are falling into. As the kids grow, the father becomes more distant from parenting responsibilities; he feels more inept, and the mom looks at him that way. It eventually leads to moms who feel the weight of the household on their shoulders and dads who feel left out. Worse than that, the kids don't have two parents working together for their benefit. It trickles down into dysfunction. Whose fault is it? I would like to say it is clearly one over the other, but it isn't.

Moms have been programmed by society to raise kids. They grow up playing with baby dolls, pushing play strollers, and tending to the cooking of plastic foods in plastic kitchens. Us guys? We are trading baseball cards and shooting each other with Transformers. What the heck do we know about kids? The truth is this: it is easy for families to fall into this trap and for the dad to be a footnote.

> The father in that situation does less, learns less, and feels less capable of providing daily care. When that pattern becomes too strong, mothers feel over-burdened, fathers feel left out, and children miss the benefits that come from having two loving, involved parents. (Gloria Ferguson BA, CAPS, Health Educator)

At first, it's a dad passing on the diaper duty, but eventually, it can lead to a great divide. How do we overcome this? The jobs of caregiving and parenting must be shared at all levels. Getting up with babies at night and handling fights between siblings should be handled in turns. If one parent is feeling overworked, he or she needs to speak up.

Children benefit from parents who are ready to roll up their sleeves and handle the parenting responsibilities that are presented to them. That being said, moms need to give dads some room to learn. Most wives have no problem allowing their husbands time to learn how to change diapers, give baths, and feed their babies, but some have trouble giving up control. Husbands in these relationships need to set ground rules. "Don't help me even if I am doing it wrong—I need to learn." That is a good mantra. *Dad 2.0* can't be passive anymore.

Are Women Naturally Better Parents?

I can tell you from experience that there are some people who are skeptical of a dads parenting chops. They are what I like to call *fools*. They look at you wondering, *Can he really give that baby a bottle?* It ain't rocket science. Place bottle at or near child's mouth. Let them feast on the contents of the bottle until they need to burp. Burp 'em. Rinse and repeat. If we can memorize all the penalty calls in hockey or the special team players on most of the teams in the NFL, then taking care of kids is easy.

There are people that claim women are programmed to be parents or that being a caregiver is women's work. A lot of people even think that being a dad is learned. Fellas, that's a myth. Men are just as capable as parents as women are. We have two hands to change diapers with. We have shoulders for babies to burp undigested formula. We have feet to walk back and forth on as we try and get our babies to go to sleep. Sure, the women have us beat in the lactating-breast department, but seriously—that's it.

What the women have in the breast department, dads more than make up in other areas. If you choose to be a full-time dad, or if you are just very involved in your kid's lives—stand tall and take pride in your contribution. Studies have suggested the following braggable benefits:

- In the typical stay-at-home-dad arrangement, the influence of the mom and dad are equal.

  o In the typical stay-at-home-mom arrangement, the influence of the dad is much less significant.
  o Dads today value their influence on their families more than in the past.

- Dads are better at teaching children to manage their bodies and emotions.

  o Moms reassure.
  o Dads encourage children to work through their problems.
  o Dads are better at teaching children to be problem solvers.

- Dads are better at teaching children how to play.
- Dads are better at teaching children how to be social and confident in a wide variety of situations.
- Dads engaged from the beginning of a child's life give children more confidence and stability.
- Dads interact with children with more variety.

- ○ Dads pick up their children differently each time.
- ○ There are less predictable outcomes of playtime.
- ○ There is more leniency at playgrounds and parks.

(As researched by Dr. Kyle D. Pruett of the Yale Child Studies Center and author of *Fatherneed* and *Partnership Parenting*.)

So don't sweat it. If you are a stay-at-home dad or a dad who wants to be active in your children's lives than that's a good thing for your family.

If you are a stay-at-home dad you should be proud of yourself and what that means for your family. Your wife can focus on her career, which will give her a lot of satisfaction and esteem. Your children will have their dad at their beck and call, which is only to their benefit. Your kids will also have a mom who comes home from work ready to pick up the parenting reins.

The truth of the matter is that kids benefit from having a dad home full-time. First, they will see a dad model to them what it means to be a good man. They will see a man who treats his wife with respect. They will experience a dad who is man enough to swallow his ego and raise his children. Being a full-time dad will have a tremendous impact on your kids as they grow and begin to have relationships of their own. Basically, stay-at-home dads make the world a better place.

When I decided to become a stay-at-home dad, my ego took a hit. It was tough on me, but looking back, I don't think any guy who makes that choice should ever feel that way. Take pride in your role. Being a stay-at-home dad is a good thing.

Stop Whining: Mastering Babies

"The rest is gravy," my dad's dad, Grandpop Schatz, always said that. He was the oldest of five. He watched his mother die of tuberculosis when he was twelve. She was so weak in her dying months that he had to carry her around the house. After she passed away, he helped raise his brothers and sisters. He dropped out of middle school just to take care of the family. In a way, he was an acting stay-at-home dad, so I could say that I really wasn't the first atypical dad in our family.

It's difficult to compare myself to my grandfather on other accounts, but I can totally relate when he used to say, "The rest is gravy." He said that because he saw a whole lot of life from his childhood years to serving in WWII. Everything that came after that was *gravy* to him.

Pregnancy wasn't a given for Jodi and me, so just having kids was amazing. We didn't care if we had boys, girls, or some other third kind of *hybrid kid;* we just wanted a healthy baby—the rest was gravy. So that is the attitude I took into my first year as a stay-at-home dad. No whining; no excuses—get it done. I didn't whine (much), you can ask my wife, but my first year as a stay-at-home dad was definitely my hardest.

After the baby comes and the family and friends stop visiting and eventually your wife returns to work, the house becomes really quiet. I mean, the baby will be crying, the dishwasher, washer, and dryer will be running, and you might have the radio on all the time; but, yeah, the house gets quiet when it's just the two of you. Like being on a desert island, at first you are just settling down and making a camp—getting the lay of the land. A few months in, you start talking to yourself. After a year, you have named and became close friends with all the trees; you don't notice that you are naked most of the time, and you have taken to walking backward everywhere just to pass the time. The first year at home with a baby is like that—kind of.

You might be asking, "How do I go about getting the 'lay of the land' with a baby?" Babies are tough because they are incessant, but really—they are uncomplicated and easy to figure out. Here are some key things I had to master the month after we came home from the hospital and some ways to make even the mundane tasks fun.

Baby Food: Bottles and Boobs

Babies are pretty clueless in the beginning when it comes to eating. A baby cries for four reasons: when they are hungry, tired, need to burp, or when they are just pissed off. When a baby is crying, it becomes pretty obvious why they are crying, depending on what time of day it is. If a crying baby was a case for a police detective, they would have it solved in like five minutes.

"So you're saying the baby woke up half an hour ago?" an officer asks.

"Yes, officer," you reply.

"The baby has been crying for how long?"

"Five minutes."

"Did you feed the baby?"

"Yes."

"Did you burp the baby?"

"Yes."

"Did you change the baby's diaper?"

"No."

"Case closed. Son, change that diaper." The officer turns and addresses some other policemen on the scene. "OK, fellas, pack it up. I hear there is a three-month-old crying at 1325 West Third Street."

Typically, when babies get out of the hospital, they are breast-fed for the first few months. Sometimes breast-feeding is a supplemental deal, and other times, it is a baby's only source of nutrition. Most stay-at-home dads don't breast-feed their children because it's impossible. So it would stand to reason, full-time breast-feeding usually stops around the time the wife returns to work. Some families do go the whole breast-pump route with the mom pumping breast milk while at work and then putting it in the fridge or freezer for later consumption.

Just thinking about that is a little weird to me. What is the typical work transaction like?

"Hey, Stan [*The sound of a mechanical device (breast pump) can be heard in the background*], can you get me that report by one thirty? I need it for my two o'clock meeting," a woman pumping says.

"Um, what did you say?" Stan replies, having trouble hearing over the humming of the pump.

"I said I need the report by one thirty," she repeats.

"I need to report by one thirty? For what?" Stan is lost.

"No, Stan, **the report**. I need *the report* by one thirty."

"I can't hear you. There's some noise—I'll just come to your desk."

"No, I'll send you an e-mail . . . Stan?" It's too late, Stan's on his way.

Reaching her desk, Stan rounds the corner, "Oh, sweet Moses! What are you doing over here?"

With our first child, Jodi pumped at work. It just sounds weird reading that sentence—"Jodi pumped at work." For our next two daughters, Jodi breast-fed for about two months and then we switched over to formula. She wasn't a big fan of the whole pumping thing, and breast-feeding isn't the easiest thing in the world for women—it hurts. A woman during her pregnancy is complaining—and rightfully so—about so many things that her body is doing to her. After the pregnancy, you will get a steady dose of complaining revolving around her boobs. You will hear things like:

"My nipples are sore" or "My nipples are chaffing" or "Ah! It hurts when the milk comes in!"

But the breast milk is good for the baby. After delivery, lactation consultants inform you and your wife about the benefits of *breast milk*. I think of all the job titles in the world that I have come across, "lactation consultant" is the funniest, but I digress.

There's a lot of irony when it comes to breast-feeding. For the last nine months of pregnancy, sex has been hard to come by if not impossible. Now you have this new baby in the picture, and it is already getting to third base. Meanwhile, us guys are still just bystanders.

Now, bottles are right up my alley. It's kind of like being a mad scientist. You are measuring out specific amounts of powders and, liquids, warming mixtures to precise temperatures, and the result is a *"formula."* Try to think of making bottles that way when you're doing it at three in the morning—it makes the process way more bearable. Like you are Dr. Jekyll's lab assistant. I always thought bottles were easy if not fun to make, but washing them has always sucked.

Burping the Baby

Babies are cool because, first and foremost, they can get away with burping. It is somehow cute when they do it. I burp *all the time,* and it is *always* gross—ask my wife. I personally like burping the baby, and I think a good thing to remember is that burping needs to happen during a feeding. If a baby doesn't burp during a feeding—keep trying. They are just being stingy.

The "Pat" Method

A burp can come from the simple tap, tap, tap that you give them on the back. Fellas, we're not trying to beat the kid senseless, but at the same time, we aren't brushing them with a feather. Start off with light pressure and slightly increase it as you tap. Go for a rhythm. *Tap-tap-TAP-rest-tap-tap-TAP-rest.* The all caps taps are slightly harder. Get a song in your head, preferably something with a good beat.

"Well, shake it up, baby, now"—you look down at your baby—"twist and shout." Still no burp. "C'mon, c'mon, c'mon, c'mon, baby, now"—nothing—"come on and work it on out."

Burp. Mission complete.

Remember, this is your baby. You down with hip-hop? Maybe you're a folksy sort of guy? Got a song in your head and can't get rid of it? Pat it out. Also, I suggest that you have some fun with the burping process; drink a soda while you feed your baby, and try and coordinate burps together. If you can't bond over burping then I don't know what to tell you.

Spit Up

Let's not be naive, burping a baby means they are going to spit up on you. Have a towel over your shoulder where you do the burping. Why a towel? Because burp cloths are stupid. They aren't even close to big enough. What type of towel? Beach towel? Bath towel? Poncho? What you'll need for this operation is a hand towel or kitchen towel—basically anything that goes over the shoulder and has some decent thickness.

Burp cloths are thin, not very absorbent, and are really just there for show.

Remember the *false finish*

A *false finish* is when a baby seems like they have stopped burping and spitting up, but in actuality, they are just taking their time. Lying dormant is a monster, **rogue burp** complete with massive amounts of spit-up. Being patient pays off.

Rogue Spit-Up

Spit-up isn't predictable. Granted most of the spit-up comes during or right after a feeding, some of it though plays hard to get. There are no warning signs for a dormant, rogue spit-up—it just happens. Rogue spit-up can happen as quickly as five minutes after a feeding or up to fifteen to twenty minutes later.

My worst spit-up story revolves around a rogue spit-up event. I was watching my niece, and I had finished feeding her over ten minutes earlier. We were sitting on the couch, and I starting giving her a couple playful tosses in the air.

"Whoaaa!" I said, giving her a toss, "Wooooooo!" I said as I caught her. At my third whoa, I looked up and was greeted with spit raining down on me. It went all over my face, my neck, my shirt—and yes—down my throat! *She spit up into my throat.* I don't know how I caught her. It all happened so fast. When I caught her, she got the spit-up all over her hands and outfit. We were both covered in nastiness.

You have been warned. Be wary of the rogue spit-up.

Bobblehead Babies

I have already suggested that instead of burp clothes you use something larger and thicker like a hand towel or kitchen towel to throw over your shoulder when you are burping your kid, but those don't work 100 percent of the time. Why? Babies have *bobbleheads*. They are desperately trying to figure out how to control their head movement, and they scarcely have the strength to do so, thus, they bobble. This erratic movement means that spit-up can potentially go almost anywhere. I have had it go down my arms, down my shirts, on my face, and in my hair.

You will learn that as long as kids are drinking a large portion of their diet, they are prone to spitting up. Whether they are drinking formula, breast milk, or ordinary milk, some of that will come back up. When it comes back up, it has to go somewhere—on you. Be ready, be vigilant, and be cautious.

Vomit

A kid vomiting is really difficult to take. The smell of bile almost instantly sets off a gag reflex for me. And babies just don't go and open the toilet like any normal person would if they are about to throw up—they simply stop what they are doing and toss cookies. Here is a typical vomit scenario:

Setting: Family Room

Time: 10:00 AM

Characters: Stay-at-home parent and baby

Plot: You are watching a TV program with your child on the couch. Your child acts and appears well. Without warning, your child turns his head slightly in your direction, perhaps to ask for help, and unleashes a spray of vomit to rival the girl from the *Exorcist*. You are now covered in vomit, your child is crying, the couch is dissolving in stomach acid, and the day is barely under way.

It doesn't get easier either. As my kids have grown older, I still hate vomit. It is such a novelty act of the human body that they really never see it coming, and the result is always the same: tons of laundry, vomit in the hair, and crying kids. I am very compassionate when one of my girls gets sick. I am like a vomit fireman—while others are running from it, I run toward it, and that's part of being a good dad in my mind.

Getting Sleep

As far as your sleep schedule, I wish I could tell you that it would be the same as before the baby. I wish I could tell you that each night you will get eight hours of restful sleep. I wish I could tell you that you will wake rested each morning with a smile on your face—but I can't. You will be awake in the middle of the night, and because you are staying home with the child, you are the designated "getter."

"Waaahh!" the baby starts crying. It's 2:30 AM.

"The baby's crying, can you **get** her?" your wife asks, waking you from a dead sleep.

"Sure, no problem. I'll **get** her. Go back to sleep," you say.

You are the **getter**. You **get** the baby, you **get** the diaper, and you **get** the bottle—it's all yours. The one positive thing about being the **getter** is that you can catch up on B movies. After around two o'clock in the morning, the only things on TV are infomercials, *Girls Gone Wild*, ad spots, and B movies. Fellas, don't watch *Girls Gone Wild* ads while feeding a baby—it's just wrong. Infomercials are acceptable as long as you are making fun of the pitchmen and the actors, but even those have entertainment limitations. This leaves B movies as the only real choice. If it weren't for my daughters, I would have never seen such classic films, such as *The Postman*, *Water World*, and *Battlefield Earth*. The more ridiculous the acting and plot, the more likely I am to stay awake—it's formulaic.

In the very early going, during breast-feeding, babies will cluster feed and are up and down a lot. It is exhausting, but it's good for the baby. Some folks will decide to continue to breast-feed for longer periods of time than others and that's totally cool. The point is, if your family decides to keep breast-feeding until your kids are talking in complete sentences or getting their high school diplomas—it's up to you, and you shouldn't worry about what anyone else thinks. I realized a long time ago that if someone has a problem with a women breast-feeding at home or in public, then they have some growing up to do.

As far as supplementing breast milk with formula—that is also a choice. For us, we found that our kids slept through the night faster with a belly full of formula than with a half-full breast-fed belly.

Also, I suggest you talk it over with your wife, but you should set up alternating sleep-in weekends. Every other weekend should be a "catch-up" weekend for either you or her. On those weekends, one parent sleeps in and the other takes the reins. This system really helped Jodi and me through the more difficult early years with each of our children and through some of those Saturday mornings following a date night.

Diapers: Stop and Smell the Roses

Diapers pose so many problems. As the diaper changer, you will witness unimaginable carnage. From getting peed and even pooped on to all the different kinds of diapers you can expect to see, changing diapers is not for the faint of heart.

Sure it's tough on the senses, but there are ways to make the process a little easier on you, *the diaper changer*. You are probably wondering, *How in God's green kingdom can diaper changing become anything remotely close to acceptable?* Truly, there is very little you can do to make the process less disgusting, but if you can change your attitude toward a dirty diaper—that's a victory in itself.

Thank the Diaper

When you are changing a truly awful diaper, try to remember that babies are a miracle. Just think, before you know it, the diapers will be gone. They will be all grown up. They will be dating and asking for the keys to the car. So "thank the diaper." I'm not advocating that you document changing diapers so you can look back fondly on them; but I'd look around because, before you know it, the baby shampoo will be gone, the crib will be packed up, and the innocence will be a thing of the past. This technique is more of a Zenlike approach to changing diapers. This Jedi mind trick doesn't always work, and results may vary.

The Pit Stop Method

I am not a big NASCAR fan, but I do know that a pit stop has to be done quickly to be of any value. The same principles apply here as well. Use a stopwatch when you're changing diapers. Create a time chart and hang it near the changing table. Use the chart to record your times and your wife's times. This chart could help settle arguments.

"Honey, I'm pretty sure you picked the movie last time, which would make this week my choice," your wife says.

"Sweetheart, last week we watched *Fried Green Turnips* or whatever—I can't handle another week of that nonsense. Don't you remember?" you plead your case.

"No, that was the week before." She is insistent.

"Then what did we watch this past week?"

"*Dark Knight*. We watched *Dark Knight*," she answers.

"That was like a month ago!" This conversation is going nowhere, and you know it. "I guess we will have to settle this with the chart. Who has the fastest time this week?" You walk over and look at the chart. "Well, looky here—with a time of 12.7 seconds . . . shoot"—your pause acknowledges your defeat—"what movie did you say you wanted again?"

Who is better at taking care of the baby? Who is the better at changing diapers? Better? I don't know who is better, but I do know who is faster—check the chart. That's all that really matters when it comes to diapers. You could offer prizes for fastest times of the year, quarterly, etc.

Diapers aren't exactly as diverse as snowflakes, but there are many different kinds of diapers that you will come across. I'm not talking brand names, sizes, or styles—I am talking about what's inside them. It all starts with the sticky, black meconium nonsense that takes like a million wipes to get off. Eventually, you will transition into the breast-milk diapers. Breast-milk diapers kind of prep you for what's to come. They are smelly, but not too smelly. They are tough to change, but not too tough. They are like *diarrhea junior*.

After the breast-milk diaper, you should expect the unexpected. Over the course of three daughters and thousands of changed diapers to my credit, I have seen it all. I have changed diapers that had pellet poop that looked like rabbit turds. There have been diapers that were green inside, there were diapers that were quite normal, and then there were those diapers that were epic. The *exploding-up-the-back diaper* is the pinnacle of diaper world.

These diapers are sloppy, hot quagmires. These diapers are full. They are so voluminous in fact that they overflow. They overflow in two main locales—up the back and down the legs. The *exploding-up-the-back diaper* means lots of laundry. It usually means cleaning crib sheets, blankets, and outfits. The exploding diapers also mean bath time. It is a wholesale event that affects every fiber of your existence.

My Worst Diaper Story

The *exploding-up-the-back diaper* has always given me fits. I remember my first one happened during one of Bella's naps. When she woke up, I noticed something was different right away. The smell was intense, but the footed pj's she was wearing were discolored in the back and in the legs. Also, the crib sheets were spotted with *brown juice*. Something new and epic had happened here. After changing the sheets and putting the dirty clothes in the washing machine, I gave Bella a bath. I thought what just happened was an aberration: one of those once in a lifetime kind of freakish diapers. Then, it happened again. The next time was in the middle of the night. Still, at least, I was at home; and I could just take care of everything in the comfort of our house.

One day, Bella and I were out running errands. We had finished almost all of our stops, and we were en route to the pediatrician. That's when I smelled something coming from the backseat. I heard an occasional noise or eruption. I thought nothing of it at the time, and I dismissed it as the typical diaper. Then we arrived at our destination—the doctor's office. It was her nine-month appointment. When I grabbed her up out of the car seat, I noticed a wet feeling on my arm. Instinctively, I knew what it was; but looking down, I was shocked to see brown juice! Sick!

Her outfit was completely covered as was the car seat. A car seat somehow intensifies the effects of *exploding-up-the-back diaper*—funneling it. The poop reached all the way up to her hairline and as far down as her socks.

All I had in the diaper bag was a onesie that was about one size too small, and I was running very low on wipes. It took twenty minutes to get the ick off. As I stripped, wiped, and changed Bella, I got a ton of inquisitive looks from other parents taking their kids to their respective appointments. Using every scrap of wipe, we made it into the office, albeit late, and into the waiting room. Bella looked like a wild child, a barbarian sausage in her six-month onesie. I could only manage to get one of the snaps to cooperate. To make matters worse, all of the other kids in the waiting room had on what looked like their Sunday best. Dresses, sweaters, belts, patent leather shoes—I thought I was in the waiting room of a portrait studio. I smelled like a ball of crap, and all I kept thinking about was the ride home. The seat wasn't suitable for Bella to sit in, but there wasn't any choice. Luckily, after the appointment, I did find an old receiving blanket in the diaper bag to line the seat with, but the brown juice bled through during our thirty-minute ride home.

Getting Peed On

Here's one thing to keep in mind when you are changing diapers: babies will pee on you. Remember when you were younger and you picked up a toad only to have it pee on you because it was the toad's only defense mechanism? Now imagine a ten to fifteen pound toad. Imagine that toad has a diaper, and you need to change it because it stinks like raw sewage. Guess what happens as soon as you start to change that toad's diaper? It pees on you. Yep, toads and babies are disgusting. Babies hate the cold, and when they are cold and naked, they act out by peeing—their only defense mechanism. It is almost a rite of passage and if you don't get peed on once during your career as a dad—don't publicize the fact because those of us who have will be super pissed.

How do I avoid the pee? There are some ways to decrease the chances that you will be peed on, but avoiding it entirely is unlikely.

- Be "diaper ready."

  - When changing diapers, always have your next one in hand ready to go.
  - If you are changing a boy, put new diaper in the place of the old one seamlessly.
  - If you are changing a girl, don't be lulled into a sense of security, they can pee outwardly (much to my surprise).
  - The temperature shouldn't be too warm or cold in the changing room—it should be just right.

- Remember the first two months.

  - Infants are more likely to pee on you.
  - Infants will also try to poop on you.
  - If an infant has just pooped, open the diaper and close it again.

- Encourage pee to go in the diaper.
- Try to outsmart the pee.

- Bath time.

  - Babies love peeing in their baths.
  - Accept it.
  - Be ready to change the water.
  - Be ready to dodge the pee.

Trying to avoid baby pee is very difficult for a number of reasons. Babies make it very difficult to sleep. A lack of sleep leads to a decline in our ability to be attentive. Babies cry frantically over messy diapers. When babies cry, as parents we act quickly. Acting quickly and inattentively is exactly what the baby wants. You are an easy target and will most likely get peed on. Perhaps it's better to find comfort in the fact that millions of parents have been peed on instead of trying to avoid it entirely.

Getting Dressed

My wife and I have different philosophies when it comes to schedules. I tend to be a little more laid-back and flexible. Jodi is pretty rigid and concrete. Overall, it makes for a good balance, but sometimes we butt heads. One afternoon, Jodi called home to tell me she was about to leave work for the day.

"So how'd your day go?" she asked.

"Well, it was pretty uneventful. We did the usual things like breakfast, lunch, and nap time. We got outside for a bit, and we played in the house the rest of the time."

"Did you give Sophia a bath?"

"Yeah, I actually just gave her a bath not too long ago."

"Wait, *what time* did you give her a bath?"

"It was around four thirty."

"Don't you think that is a *little late* in the day to give her a bath?" she snapped.

I thought for a second as I was confused and replied, "It's not like she is going to work or something. I mean as long as she gets bathed eventually, isn't that the point? If she were going to school or a job interview, then I would make sure she was cleaned and ready to go first thing."

I suppose there are some positives to hiring a baby; I just don't know what they are. The drawbacks are pretty alarming; I mean, their pants are always falling down and shoes are constantly missing. Once their shoes are off, they *have* to take their socks off. They seem to do strange things like put stickers on cats or put their hand inside a cup of milk and cry after they get wet. They spend a large amount of time lying on the floor and spitting up. They are always begging for food and drinks or asking to be picked up or put down. Now why should I worry what time they get bathed? I know they don't care.

Dressing the Baby

A baby requires clothing, but for some reason, they despise socks. To be fair, I hate socks too, but this chapter isn't about me. Babies kick their socks off *all the time*. A baby does this for any number of reasons. They like to see you pick up stuff, they like to show that they can control some portion of their lives no matter how small it is, or they just hate socks. Don't sweat the socks—they are optional. As long as your house is somewhat warm, socks aren't important. Go for comfort. Nothing too tight, nothing too hot, no leather pants, no feather boas—basically nothing a rock star would wear.

Dressing a baby is really silly and fun. They don't really know how to move, so they just accept whatever you put on them. Like I said, remember comfort—but the style choices are all you. Stripes and plaids, fluorescent orange jumpsuits, or a baby-sized mechanic shirt with the baby's name spelled out on it—get creative. Express yourself with your kids while you can because soon they will be able to think for themselves—and move their limbs better.

Some really cool Web sites to check for hip, nontraditional baby clothes are the following:

http://www.thinkgeek.com/geek-kids/newborn-infant/
http://store.rebelinkbaby.com/
http://www.punkbabyclothes.net/

In my mind, nothing says I have a cool baby like a camouflage onesie.

Giving the Baby a Bath

Babies get dirty. They poop in their pants. They pee in their pants. They spit up *all the time*. Their noses run like a faucet, and they routinely smear the boogers on their face, in their hair, and on their hands and arms. Basically, babies have no self-control whatsoever. If I peed my pants, I would be in the shower as quick as I could get my clothes off, but babies couldn't care less. Most folks say you don't have to bathe babies every single day—but seriously, they need it.

The best thing about giving babies a bath is the ***just-been-bathed baby smell***. I contend that the ***just-been-bathed baby smell*** rivals *new car* smell and *freshly painted house* smell. There are a number of reasons why the ***just-been-bathed baby smell*** is so great. First, up until their bath, the baby has smelled of dried formula and urine. Second, you don't cuddle a car. Lastly, it makes you feel good. A clean baby is a reminder of a job well done.

How to Wrap a Baby in a Receiving Blanket

I would like to say that I am a baby-wrapping expert, but I'm not. The honest truth is that I really don't think anyone is. Why? Because as soon as you think you have your kid wrapped up tight—they get loose. Also, babies are humans. Like all humans, babies tend to move around. Although babies do like to be swaddled, they also like to be free. Here's a step-by-step on how to tuck your child into a receiving blanket:

- Google "how to swaddle a baby."
- Try the technique described.
- Watch as your baby squirms free in less than ten minutes.
- Swaddle the baby again.
- This time they free themselves almost immediately.
- Give up.

When you google "how to swaddle a baby," you will find there are a ton of videos and Web sites dedicated on showing folks how to correctly *swaddle*. For some reason, I don't like the word *swaddle*. *Swaddling* is what moms do in between scrapbooking sessions. Dads, they *wrap*. Another good resource is the labor and delivery nurse. They cover the correct *baby-wrapping* technique and love teaching dads how to do anything baby related, so pay attention.

I am convinced that receiving blankets are a racket. Why? Because most receiving blankets aren't big enough. Receiving blankets are absurd. They were invented to keep the baby feeling secure, warm, and *tucked in*; but they never work as designed. Swaddling is only really necessary for the first few months of a baby's life anyway, so by the time you figure it out, it will most likely be obsolete. The best advice I can give you is to buy bigger receiving blankets and not to stress over it *too much*.

Your life around the house will revolve around baby chores. Befriend them. Do not resist becoming the ultimate dad. Being a good dad is

your job, and your successes are measured here by the health and happiness of your baby. There are a lot of people that think dads can't do this stuff, but that simply isn't true. Not only can we handle babies, but we can also be dominant caregivers.

Section 3
The Experienced Parent

I remember when Jodi and I were first-time parents—rookies. We were predictably vigilant monitoring dropped bits of food like guards at a prison diving to stop escapees. Three-second rule? That was about three seconds too long in our house. Were we overprotective? Nah. Well, maybe just a bit.

We limited the number of times we drove with Bella—car accidents happen, you know. We limited what Bella could listen to. She could only listen to classical music and nothing heavy—Mozart, Bach, and *maybe* Beethoven. We limited the number of times we took her out of the house—smallpox. No matter how much she cried during Mass, we made it each week to church—fear of demonic possession.

I feel first-time parents are beset with fear. We think that we are going to mess up and take all the precautions and try to foolproof every action we take. First-time parents are sometimes more like secret service agents than parents. Instead of checking rooftops for snipers, we are putting bumpers on coffee table corners.

With each passing month and, invariably, with each passing child, I have become more of a realist. The three-second rule began to fade. I remember with Mady we were still pretty protective, but we weren't frantically snatching dirty food from her mouth like we did with Bella. A little dirt, we discovered, wasn't the end of the world. By the time Sophia entered the picture, the three-second rule was way gone. I remember her finding a petrified chicken nugget in her car seat one day when we were running errands. I didn't bat an eye as she crunched down on the week-old piece of pressed chicken. *Hey, it's protein.*

When we were expecting Isabella, we intently read books, magazines, articles, leaflets, flyers, fortune cookies, really anything you could read about parenting as we readied ourselves to deal with the rigors of infants and toddlers. Here is a quick synopsis of what the books say: as babies get older, they grow, eat more food, and do more stuff (i.e., walking, talking, testing your cabinet latches).

These books said nothing about getting three kids into the car in less than fifteen minutes. These books never told me that I would feel isolated as a stay-at-home parent. These books didn't tell me that toddlers hate restaurants. There were lots of problems I had to solve on my own. This section gives you insight into the areas of parenting that gave me the most trouble. This section gives you firsthand accounts of stay-at-home-dad parenting drama. This section gives you practical advice and philosophies to help you on your parenting journey. This section, most of all, hopes to turn you into an ***experienced parent***.

Rinse and Repeat: Dealing with Monotony

My dad always says, "Remember whose shoulders you stand on," which is usually followed by a long narrative about my grandfathers and my great-grandfathers. Being a dad now myself, I can't help but think of my dad and my grandfathers and their challenges. Interestingly enough, my Grandpop Hlatki had a similar experience to that of my Grandpop Schatz. He lost his mother at an early age while he was living in Czechoslovakia. He eventually made it to the United States and Baltimore where he became a dad five times over, and like me, he had all daughters. Grandpop Hlatki worked for years at Bethlehem Steel. He worked the swing shift. It was hard, draining work that kept him from his family more than he would have liked. He told me one of his biggest regrets was the long hours he worked and how he wished he could have been around his daughters more.

I, on the other hand, get to be around my daughters all the time. Sure, my occupation can be tough at times, but I'm not working in a steel mill. My work hazards are nasty diapers not molten steel. No matter how tough things get at home, I realize that I have it good. That's the value of recognizing where you come from. With that in mind, I look at my minor challenges as being exactly that—minor.

So far, we have covered the basics of babies—what's next? One of the bigger challenges full-time parents face is the relentlessness of the stay-at-home lifestyle. Diapers roll in and collect like waves against the beach. The laundry keeps coming as do the dishes. The days start to blend together. You really notice that you have become a victim to the monotony when you have no idea what day it is. But how do we deal with monotony?

The Routine

Your routine by around month three may have become sadly predictable. By now, you have become accustomed to your baby napping at the same time every day. Your feeding schedule and diaper changes happen with military precision. There is nothing wrong with a finely tuned schedule. Babies thrive when they know the routine. Babies also can adapt. Babies can nap in Pack n Plays. Babies can nap during car trips. Babies can nap in strollers. Babies can be fed almost anywhere, and as long as you have a relatively flat surface, you can change a baby's diaper.

I have seen parents who are too rigid with their schedules, and I think it has a negative impact on their lives. The first time I realized how debilitating a baby-focused schedule could be was when we invited some neighbors over for dinner when Bella was around six months old. We suggested six o'clock.

"Six?" an anxious mom asked.

"Yeah, we normally eat around six—is that *too* early?" I responded.

"Actually, it's *too* late. Sally just *has* to be in bed by six-thirty. She goes to bed *every night* at six-thirty," the mom insisted.

"Well, Bella doesn't go to bed until eight-thirty or nine—you can just use her crib if you like," I offered.

"No, Sally is very particular. If she isn't in her crib, she just won't sleep."

"OK, well, I guess we could have dinner at four."

"That would be great! We normally eat at three-thirty, but four will work fine."

See how ridiculous that sounds? Seriously, how can babies be particular? I can understand a seventy-five-year-old man being set in his ways—he has had time to grow accustomed to living life a certain way. But babies? Nope. They are fresh out of the womb. Some babies are particular, but it's their parents that infuse limits and restrictions to what a baby can adapt to. Don't get caught in that trap of conforming to the baby. A baby can't tell you what to do. You are like two hundred pounds heavier and way more dexterous. You make the rules for the schedule.

In my opinion, babies shouldn't be tiptoed around. I think you should do things like vacuum during naptimes and play music just so a baby can get used to sleeping through the din of everyday life. And guess what, they get used to sleeping through noisy conditions almost immediately. Seriously, just being out of the womb is much quieter than what was going on inside. Short of exploding munitions outside of their rooms, there isn't much that should wake a baby when they are sleeping.

Just remember it's **your** schedule and not to set the precedent that you are willing to be a slave to your child's timetable. Work around the problems a baby presents, and think outside of the box. Parents who schedule themselves into a box mean well, but I'm here to tell you that they are wrong. I am not saying that you switch your kids to midnight shift every other week just to check their tolerance, but all three of our kids have grown accustomed to the fact that the schedule that is most important is the one that works best for **everyone**. Just remember, babies are wonderful at adapting if you allow them the chance. They can sleep virtually anywhere and through just about any commotion—it all depends on what you expose them to. Now it's time to add some variety to your daily routine.

Music

Nowhere is it written that a normal day at home has to be lame. Music can turn an otherwise bland day into a fun one for everyone involved. I actually installed a speaker in the ceiling of Bella's room and piped classical music in while she napped during the day. I am not sure what music you listen to, but I do know that babies pretty much hate super loud anything. Here are some **dos** and **don'ts**:

- Do play music at a reasonable decibel level.
- Do play music that is soothing to both of you (your baby will help you decide).
- Do play music while your baby naps (the sooner your baby learns to sleep with ambient noise the better).
- Do let the baby see you dance.
- Do dance with the baby.
- Do set the baby up ASAP in a bouncer seat to see them dance.
- Do give a baby a rattle to shake while you listen to music.
- Don't set your baby up in a swing and invite your old band over for a jam session.

- Don't listen to gangster rap or heavy metal—avoid traumatizing the baby.

Seriously, I knew this baby that listened to gangster rap with his dad, and he was always walking around with pants hung low, diaper out—it had to be the music.

Let music be a metaphor to how you run your household. It's really all up to what your personal preferences are. Think about ways to make daily life more exciting. Maybe you always wanted to teach yourself the guitar or the piano. Maybe you love to read. Get some use out of your library card. Educate yourself on topics you always wanted to. In a way, being a stay-at-home parent is like being Bill Murray in *Groundhog Day*. *What would you do if every day was the same?*

Isolation: Getting Out of the House

Isolation isn't your baby's fault. They are kind of limited and unapologetic for being, well, babies. Let's face it; babies are cute, harmless, loveable creatures, but terrible at holding conversations.

"Did you see the game last night?" you ask your baby.

"Ppppplllllllbbbbbbbbbbbbbb." Your baby, looking at a rattle cross-eyed, responds by blowing air over its tongue.

"Yeah, but did you see the *end*?" you ask excitedly.

"Mmmmmmmeeeehhhhhhhhhhhhhhh?" Your baby drops the rattle and starts trying to get it—hands flailing.

"Right, so why didn't they just call a time-out?" you say in agreement.

"Ehh. Ehhhhh. EHHHHHHHHHHHHHHH!" Your baby starts crying.

"I know, but there's always next year," you say, consoling your baby. "Up top!" You ask for a high five. Sadly, you are left hanging.

Before long, you will find yourself desperate for adult interaction. Let's face it; a baby's schedule can almost force your hand, making you stay inside day after day. It isn't strange if you begin to feel resentment toward your baby—it happens. Not only do stay-at-home dads have a tough time with isolation but so do stay-at-home moms. That's why it is crucial for you and your baby's sake to set the right precedent. You need to become mobile.

Think about it. Do you want your stay-at-home identity to be that of a *homebody* stuck inside day after day? Wouldn't you rather be nimble?

Your day doesn't need to revolve only around your baby—it is a *team routine*. Sure they need to be fed, changed, and take naps—but why can't those things happen outside of the house?

Probably the first thing to remember when you are preparing for a day outside the house is how to pack a diaper bag. When you are packing a diaper bag, you are *packing for freedom*. If you forget something, like diapers, you will eventually need to get them, and momentarily, *relinquish your freedom*. A great idea is to have a checklist. It's akin to a military maneuver. Accuracy, speed, and thoroughness are rewarded.

The Ultimate Diaper Bag Checklist

- ☐ Bottle (Remember a backup bottle if you plan on being gone for a while.)
- ☐ Formula (There are containers that hold premeasured amounts of formula just for such outings, or you can go with the store-bought premeasured plastic sleeves, but they *cost more*.)
- ☐ Water for formula (You can pack bottled water and one empty baby bottle or multiple bottles prefilled with water ready for a formula.)
- ☐ Sippy cups with juice (if they are old enough)
- ☐ Cold pack (Most diaper bags come with an insulated compartment for storing bottles to keep them cool, but if you plan on being out for a while, a cold pack is a good idea.)
- ☐ Food (If they are old enough for solid food, Cheerios, Goldfish, Teddy Grahams are great toddler snacks.)
- ☐ Swiss Army knife or Leatherman (in case you need to erect a shelter, light a fire, build a raft, etc.).
- ☐ First-aid kit (for you, your baby, or if you need to make a field dressing for a stranger in need—you are kind of like a medic).
- ☐ Iodine-based water tablets (used in case you decide to stay outdoors overnight and need to drink stream water)
- ☐ Toys (for babies: rattles, binkies, stuffed animals, dangly toys that hang from a car seat's handle; for toddlers: crayons, coloring books, stuffed animals, books)
- ☐ Diapers (Try to keep five to ten diapers in your bag at all times.)

- ☐ Bags to put dirty diapers in (Sometimes you won't be near a trash can when you change a diaper)
- ☐ Wipes (Buy two large plastic cases to hold wipes—one stays home; one for the diaper bag—keep both stocked.)
- ☐ Clothes (Have two backup outfits that are seasonally appropriate. A good tip is to have them in a gallon plastics storage bag—soiled clothes go into the storage bag when you change them.)
- ☐ One change of clothes for you (You never can be too prepared, Boy Scout.)
- ☐ Changing pad (You don't ever want to change your kid on a dirty floor in a public restroom without one. No matter how many paper towels you put down—it still seems nasty.)
- ☐ Snack for you
- ☐ Drink for you
- ☐ Cell phone
- ☐ MP3 player

A Note on Diaper Bags

Much of what's out there is made for the ladies. Flowers, Pooh Bear, paisley, and pastels are the industry standards. I remember when I picked out a diaper bag in the spring of 2000; I had to concede to use the *Pooh Bear bag.* My feelings were that all bears have a *don't-mess-with-me* side and that was kind of manly. There isn't a huge industry for diaper bags guys can use without cringing, but thankfully, some folks are starting to make some really great stuff. Here are a few Web sites to check out if you are looking for a bag that won't offend your senses:

- http://www.dadgear.com/
- http://www.diaperdude.com/
- http://www.drmoz.com/

The *diaper-bags-made-for-men* industry is in its infancy. I only wish that these bags had been around when my kids were little. Also, you probably have a decent, nonpaisley diaper bag in your house right now that you could use. What is a diaper bag anyway? A bag with pockets, zippers, and mesh, right? Backpacks are great diaper bags and are way better suited for guys.

Why Do We Feel Isolated?

For me, it wasn't long before I needed to get out of the house. This sort of isolation is really strange. You really aren't *isolated.* You are just cooped up in your house. It's not like you are perched on top of a mountain or on an island in the middle of the ocean. You aren't even *alone.* You're just home with your *baby.* Still you feel cut off. Why?

Well, for starters, up until this point in your life you have been surrounded by a peer group of your maturity level. Babies aren't exactly mature. The way they interact with their world is to put stuff in their mouths. They are consistently astonished by peekaboo, and at the drop of a hat, they are either sleeping or wailing.

Another reason why full-time parents can start to feel isolated is the fact that a day with a baby isn't exactly super exciting. A day at home is repetitive, mundane, and downright boring. Months go by, and seemingly, the only changes you notice in your baby are the size of their diapers. Babies are also not as physically capable as their parents. They can't throw a football or catch a baseball. Babies can't play one-on-one basketball—they aren't ballers. Even trash talk won't get your baby to play better D, they just don't care.

"That's right!" you yell as you make yet another layup while your baby watches from the comfort of its bouncy seat. "What now, baby?"

"Hiiinnnn-ha!" Your baby does a little baby jump in excitement.

"Oh, *that's* all day long. I got plenty more where that came from," you say as you drive to the basket. You notice that your baby is looking down, smacking its hands against the bouncy seat.

One good thing about the isolation is that most stay-at-home parents have dealt with it at one point or another. Why is that good? Because the other moms and dads you meet out there will most likely be as desperate and anxious to talk to another adult as you are.

Your Neighborhood

Your neighborhood is a great place to go for walks. Taking your baby out for a stroll is the easiest way to get out of the house. If you live in a neighborhood with a lot of young parents, taking a stroll is a great way to talk to people you may not have had an opportunity to meet otherwise. Parents are always on the lookout for other parents, especially parents who have children that are their children's ages. Babies are icebreakers. It's funny how you don't realize it, but you are chock-full of information regarding your baby, and you have questions to ask other parents about theirs. There may be a mom or dad you meet that you would not have normally talked to unless you had a baby, and soon you are having an in-depth conversation.

"Hello," you say politely to a neighborhood mom.

"Hi," she replies. "Awww, your daughter is adorable. What's her name?"

"Thanks. This is Bella." You look at the woman's child and try to decide whether you are looking at a boy or girl. For some reason, I had real trouble figuring this one out when I was a new parent. It was about fifty-fifty for me. I would look at the baby and think—what the hell is that thing? Babies don't have any masculine or feminine features—they have baby features: baby fat, huge heads, and short arms and legs. The key is to look for the *x-factor*. The *x-factor* could be a barrette in a tiny tuft of hair, a light blue shirt, or frilly socks. Look quickly. Find the x-factor. But sometimes there is no *x-factor*. You see a baby in a white onesie, wearing a white hat.

What's even more awkward than getting the sex of a baby wrong is the use of adjectives to describe them. Moms use words like *cute, cutie, adorable, sweetie, lovely, perfect, amazing, miraculous, breathtaking, stunning, precious, angelic, darling, delightful, lovable, beautiful,* and *gorgeous.* As dads, how can we talk about babies and still keep our masculinity intact? It is a challenge. Here is a list of acceptable words to use when complimenting babies.

Acceptable words dads can use to compliment babies:

- cute
- cutie
- adorable (only to be used if you are at a complete loss for words)

After looking for the *x-factor* and remembering your available words for complimenting babies, you say something like, "Your son is a cutie, how old is he?" Your response is met with an inquisitive look.

"This is Madison—she's four months old as of yesterday." *Madison? Really? Why make it so tough on us?* you think to yourself. *Madison* is wearing a duck shirt and baby jeans.

"I was just testing you of course. She is adorable." You rebound. "Bella is fourteen weeks." On an aside, I am not sure when all parents decide to stop using weeks and switch to months to describe their child's age. Usually, I think, it's somewhere around the four-month range. Although I have heard a mom refer to her eight-month-old as thirty-four-weeks-old, most parents switch to months by then. Also, some parents feel compelled to continue using months well into year two. I am not sure if it was the same mom, but I remember hearing about a thirty-one-month-old tot. Whatever is the shortest method to describe your baby's age—go with it; otherwise, you will be making life harder on yourself and those you meet for no reason whatsoever. The conversation continues:

"Bella? I love that name. Is that short for Isabella?" the mom asks.

"Thank you. Yes, Bella is really an Isabella—we like shortening it though. Do you have any nicknames for Madison? Like Maddy?"

"Not yet. I really never liked the name Maddy, so we are sticking with Madison," the mom answers.

You are baffled as to why they would choose Madison but not like Maddy. Continuing on, you ask, "So how is she sleeping for you?"

"She is pretty colicky. Up like three times a night. But I read this story about colicky babies and how doctors have found that they might have some form of baby acid reflux or heartburn. So we are asking our pediatrician about it this week to see if there is something we can try." She opens up to you. The great thing about talking to other parents is that you can hear about what has worked for them and what hasn't. What their difficulties have been and how they have overcome them. Not everything you hear will be helpful or even applicable, but each little nugget of information is valuable. "How does Bella sleep for you and your *wife*? By the way, I'm Patty, and my husband is Bob—we live right down the street on the right."

"Hi, Patty. I'm Joe and my wife is Jodi. We live one street over on the end . . ." and you are off and running. You may not have everything in the world in common with the parents you meet, but the ones you can share a laugh with and talk about a variety of topics are the ones to remember.

The Great Outdoors

Fresh air and the sound of nature are a welcome departure from the smell of formula and the sound of *Barney & Friends*. Visiting the great outdoors is a fantastic way to break up the routine. I don't recommend rock climbing, scuba diving, or sky diving with a baby, but basic hiking isn't out of the question. The baby backpack carriers on the market are wonderful, and it is amazing how a short time outdoors reenergizes a guy.

Besides hiking, another great outdoor activity is mountain biking. I have used both the bike trailers and the attached baby seats to bring babies and toddlers with me on bike rides. Typically, the trailers are better for older babies and toddlers, but some trailers do come equipped to handle babies specifically. While attachable baby seats are cheaper, they are a bit more difficult to balance while riding, especially when you are getting on or off a bike.

What if the baby gets tired and starts crying during a hike? Walk it off. The first time is always the worst time. If a baby grows accustomed to sleeping while you're hiking, that means you are doing something right. What if the baby makes a stinky during a bike ride? You are a mobile changing station! Go to work on that diaper and keep on trucking.

Remember: Babies and sun don't mix. Use sunblock and use it often.

Grocery Stores and Shopping

OK, this might not seem like an *outlet* per se, but when confronted with another day home alone with the baby, a trip to the grocery store to find deals on *boneless-skinless chicken breasts* can be really inviting. You know what's really strange about grocery shopping? The carts. The carts are this third-party contraption that you use maybe on a weekly to biweekly basis, but they are a great way to track the growth and maturity of your baby.

At first, your baby is in its car seat sitting on top of the cart. Then you start experimenting with buckling your baby directly into the cart. At first, the baby looks small and out of place in the huge shopping cart. You may even feel inclined to secure your baby with bags of flour on either side or gallons of milk. Then, all too soon, the baby is filling that little seat. They are sitting up very sturdily and starting to grab and reach for all the stuff around them. Shopping carts don't lie—your baby is growing.

Warning

By the time your baby becomes pretty stable in the shopping cart, that's about the time you will become complacent. Babies like to squirm out of seats, and a shopping cart is no exception. Stay vigilant. A lot of babies and toddlers suffer injuries each year while trying to escape shopping carts.

Classes for Infants

There are a lot of classes for infants and toddlers that are available through the local libraries or YMCAs. I have taken my share. One thing is true about these classes: *they are for the parents.*

I remember bringing my oldest daughter to *infant story time* for children ages zero to twelve months at our local library. I was a little wary of the whole experience, but Jodi encouraged me to go. "It would be good for Bella," she said. I had my doubts. First, babies have the shortest attention spans ever. Here's an example of a typical baby's thought pattern:

Foot? Hello, foot. There's my hand on my foot! Come here, hand. Huh? I want food! What's that noise? Who's that stranger? My gums hurt. How do I put my hand in my mouth again? Yeahhhhh. That's better. I like the way my hand tastes. Hand. Handddd. What's that noise? Who's talking? Where am I? Daddy!? Daddy!? Oh, there you are. Hey!? Where'd my hand go? Babies have no clue what's going on.

Back to *story time* at the library. I went once and that was more than enough for me. I got there early because I thought that meant I was being a good parent. I remember waiting for the class to start. I watched as parents and babies started to arrive. It was a spectacle. Some babies came in crying. There were moms, and there were couples. I was the only dad by himself. When the librarian started to read the story, one of the babies started crying. Apparently, that baby was a critic. Two pages into the story and half the babies were either crying or fighting to get out of their parents' laps.

At that moment, it seemed like the librarian was reading a volume of the encyclopedia. Looking back, the story took all of like ten minutes, but it was absolute bedlam. Halfway through, two parents left with crying babies, never to return. The remaining babies acted like they were on fire. I was thinking to myself, *We can do this. There are only a few more pages left, but damn, that librarian reads slowly. Lady, the babies don't care about your voice inflection that much—seriously.*

It was almost braggable that Bella wasn't thrashing around. She almost seemed like she was paying close attention to the librarian's every word. Then I realized she wasn't focusing on the librarian, she was focused on business—business in her pants.

As an aside, I think one of the funnier things to see is a baby concentrating on a bowel movement. They get still and super serious. When the story ended, everyone could smell Bella's bears. It was epic. Her diaper created this permeating smell that kind of rolled up your nose and set up camp. That's when I realized something beautiful. When you are in a public setting with other parents and babies, no one can be absolutely sure whose baby pooped. Sure, I knew what Bella had just done, but no one else did. It was our little secret. A toxic, offending secret. I kept a poker face and said good-bye and thank-you to the librarian. Bella never made a peep, but her butt told the story—no more infant story time. While Bella has always excelled at reading, I attribute little to the time when she pooped herself during infant story time.

Another class I took Bella to was an infant swimming class. If you want to be humiliated as a stay-at-home dad, by all means, attend infant swimming classes. Otherwise, I would avoid them. I would like to begin by saying, infants don't swim. Next, I would like to say that toddlers don't swim. The entire infant/toddler swimming class genre is, as far as I can tell, a racket. What is an infant swimming class like? Well, you are in a pool's shallow end in your suit and your baby is in theirs. There are about four or five moms in the pool with you with their babies and an instructor. What happens next is that you bounce around the pool singing songs like "Wheels on the Bus" and "Twinkle, Twinkle Little Star."

I had no idea there was going to be *singing*. I thought it was a *swimming* class. To make matters worse—I didn't know the words to all the songs. I felt like a bad parent because I forgot the words to "Mary Had a Little Lamb."

I did however have some good experiences in other classes. I found a cool toddler art class for our second daughter, Mady, and a great music class for our youngest, Sophia. Some of the classes are good, some are bad, and some are the stuff that nightmares are made of. Don't feel obligated to attend classes for your infant because you think it will give them a *head start*.

Philosophy

There are tons of different ways to get out of the house, but the key is to find your comfort area. Is it the hiking thing? Do you like taking day trips? Maybe you like going to a neighborhood playground. The key is to get used to getting out of the house with the kid from the start. Exposing your kids to the world is a good thing. There is no medical reason to keep babies indoors. Sure, you don't want to hang around sick people or hospital ERs, but that's just common sense. The reality is that babies and parents benefit from a change in scenery. It leads to a sense of empowerment and, eventually, confidence. I took my daughters out with me everywhere. I had no choice, but looking back, I couldn't see why I shouldn't.

Also, from a fatherly perspective, when you are out with your baby, you will get more chances to practice being a dad. You can point out clouds, flowers, and animals. You can talk to your baby about any range of topics, and it doesn't matter if you are saying the right things—the baby doesn't mind. It's all practice. The baby is practicing too. They are learning how to react to the world around them. They are figuring out your disposition and learning from your example. It's all practice when they are little. Being a dad requires practice, and practice makes perfect.

Pioneering Playgroups

The ratio of stay-at-home moms to stay-at-home dads was around 60:1 the last time I checked. Granted, there are a lot of dads who are now staying home one day a week and being a part-time at-home dad, but the statistics don't lie—stay-at-home dads are in a women's world. As a demographic, women have spent a lot of time at home. They have an entire culture—one that is about as foreign as any culture can be to the uninitiated. As stay-at-home dads, we are truly *pioneers* forging a path into *uncharted territory.* We have a responsibility to those that will come after us. This leads us to playgroups.

If you want to *branch out* as a full-time dad and actively try to fight the feelings of *isolation,* you may eventually consider joining a *playgroup.* Playgroups are the height of the *daytime culture.* Think of playgroups as *tribes of natives* in a new world. You have just built your settlement, and you are making your way into a strange new environment. As you explore the landscape, you come across factions of other cultures. Their cultures are foreign to you. Your languages are very different. You say things like *touchdown, home run, craft beer,* and *Sportscenter.* They say things like *McDreamy, Oprah,* and *I feel bloated.* What you thought was your neighborhood is actually a collection of multiple tribes of women who have branched off from one another forming unique playgroups.

What brings these women together? Why do they separate? Sometimes it is as simple as the age of their children. Sometimes it's the church they go to. Sometimes playgroups are formed regionally. Sometimes they are formed from activities or classes kids have gone to together. Sometimes they form separate groups because some ladies have been friends before they had kids, and the playgroup is just an extension of that friendship.

Enter you. This is *new ground,* so tread lightly. Each tribe is different. Some may be more *warlike* when they encounter stay-at-home dads. Some tribes may be very *welcoming and inquisitive.* Some tribes may *flee and retreat* from your presence, and sometimes you'll be the one fleeing and retreating. The fact is that you will never know until you try to become part of a playgroup.

As a rookie stay-at-home dad, I had my first experience with playgroups through a local neighborhood group called the Bagel Club. Since you have already read about it earlier in the book, I can simply say that this playgroup setting wasn't ideal for me. I felt left like the odd man out or that they were waiting for me to leave at times. Basically, a good rule of thumb is that when you have been invited to a playgroup out of obligation—don't have high hopes.

Playgroups are usually best when they are suggested. Let's say you take your child to an activity and routinely see the same moms or dads there and you quickly realize that you can hold a conversation with some of them—ask about starting a playgroup. Also, another great tip is to take your baby out on walks around the neighborhood during the day. As you push your stroller, it is truly amazing to see how many strangers come up and talk to you. The ones you enjoy talking to are the ones you ask about playgroups—not the first mom or dad who talks to you. Take your time. Patience is rewarded.

Playgroup Conversations

I was the only guy at 95 percent of all the playgroups I have ever attended. What does that mean exactly? Well, no one talks about sports, and if they do, it is only to remark about the good-looking guys on the team in question. I remember going to playgroup and bringing up the NFL and the start of the football season. Living about thirty minutes outside of Baltimore, most of the talk revolves around the Ravens. In almost a joking tone I say, "So what does everyone think about the Ravens this year?"

"Well, their new coach is pretty hot," Deb remarks. *Hot? Really?* The one time I bring up sports and the moms immediately contribute, but only about how good-looking the coaches and players are.

"What's his name?" Courtney asks.

"Harbaugh, is that right, Joe?" Deb responds. The conversation is well under way.

"Yeah, John Harbaugh, I think he will be great for the team," I tell them.

"Well, he is cute. What about Boller? He's really cute too," Deb says.

"I don't know about—" I start to say, but I am cut off.

"What about Flacco's unibrow? What's up with that?" Courtney asks.

"I know, right? If he took care of that, he wouldn't be too bad either," Deb says.

That's how playgroups go a lot of times. As a guy, you contribute, but the conversations are driven by the moms. If you are in the right group, they recognize when to get back on track.

"But the Ravens do look like they have a chance this year," Deb finishes up her statement.

Conversations with moms at playgroups can be gossipy at times. Sometimes the conversations can revolve around cute guys, sometimes the ladies will talk about their sagging breasts or maybe their love handles, but inevitably, moms will talk about their pregnancies. It seems like playgroup moms have a collective amnesia when it comes to pregnancies. They never seem to remember talking about their pregnancies. What makes pregnancy talk worse is that guys bring very little to the table.

"So, Joe, what was your pregnancy like?" A playgroup mom asks.

"Well, it was really easy. I gained some sympathy weight and told Jodi to push a few times. The sex wasn't pretty, but you know what I mean." What can a guy really offer during pregnancy talk?

Playgroup moms will talk about it all. Nothing is taboo. They also use a bunch of terms and phrases that were foreign to me when I first started frequenting playgroups. Below is list of those terms and phrases and their definitions:

- Hawt—hot, as in a guy
- McDreamy—a hot guy from a TV show
- McSteamy—a different hot guy from the same TV show
- Brad Pitt—a hot guy from the movies
- Latte—a hot coffee drink
- Starbucks—a really good store to buy hot coffee drinks
- Period—something that women get once a month
- Crampy—a description of once-a-month pains
- Retain water—something women do once a month—I think

- Outfit—something that women wear
- Ann Taylor—a store to get good outfits
- Longaberger—a basket of some importance
- Prada—a bag of importance
- Breast-feeding—something that women talk about or do during playgroup
- Sore nipples—associated with breast-feeding
- Sagging breasts—something that women get as they get older
- Contractions—painful things associated with labor and delivery
- Epidural—something given during pregnancies to reduce pain

Sure, playgroups can be an assault on our manliness, but it's all about the kids. Most moms do try to make the conversations as universal as possible, and as long as you can toss in a witty one-liner here and there, you'll be fine. If you ever feel like you are being left out intentionally, find another playgroup. There is no reason to remain where you get bad vibes. Overall though, I think most moms are ecstatic to include a dad in their group.

Hosting a Playgroup

After you join or create a playgroup, it will eventually be your turn to *host*. When you host a playgroup, most likely, you will have no clue how to prepare for your guests—no worries, I'm here to help. Here's what you'll need:

- Coffee
- Cream and sugar
- Iced tea (homemade is a bonus and usually very well received)
- Margarita mix (just in case)
- Juice (for the kids and adults—have enough)
- Kids' sippy cups (parents invariably forget to bring a cup)
- Pastries or donuts
- Bagels
- Homemade baked good (extra credit, but the reactions are worth it)
- Kids' snacks (Goldfish, cut fruit, Teddy Grahams, etc.)
- Make sure you are well stocked with wipes and diapers (parents may forget one or the other)

- Hide the toys with sentimental value (the ones your kids will get upset about sharing)

Lay out utensils and napkins. Make sure the house is clean, and toys are obvious and accessible.

Playgroups are worth all the time and effort it will take to read this chapter. Stay-at-home moms get what you are going through as a full-time parent and can become great friends. The friendships are welcome, but you can also learn from being involved in a playgroup. After all, a playgroup is a collection of parents and their kids. When you get a bunch of parents together, you can help teach each other by sharing experiences in parenting, relaying who the best pediatricians in the area are, and just by watching how everyone handles their kids.

I respect stay-at-home moms. They are just as resourceful and imaginative as any dad I have met, and I have learned a great deal from being around them. Moms handle adversity differently than dads do. They absorb so much and keep on ticking. Dads generally have a breaking point that is much easier to reach. Moms are also better at being prepared. You can't help but learn something by watching them in action. I learned to store Band-Aids in the kitchen from a mom. I learned to keep a snot rag in my pocket from a mom. I learned better ways to store snacks and toys from moms. That's the beauty of a playgroup. You get to learn some great parenting-problem-solving techniques, plus, there's the adult conversation.

On the flip side, I have noticed that I have influenced some of the moms I have been in playgroups with. The first playgroup I went to was the Bagel Club. I remember my first time there. The moms spent most of the time talking to each other almost ignoring the kids. I spent most of my time there playing with my kid and everyone else's. With each passing week at the Bagel Club, I noticed more moms playing with their kids. Maybe they saw how much fun I was having or how much fun the kids were having. For whatever reason it happened—it happened. I called it the *daddy effect*.

Dads-Only Playgroup

The *dads-only playgroup* rarely happen. I have been the only guy in almost every playgroup I have ever attended. The only exception has been the times I have been able to hang out with my brother-in-law, Jason. Jason is a work-at-home/stay-at-home dad, and we have gotten our kids together a number of times over the course of the last few years. Our playgroups revolve around two things: food and the kids. Sure we talk, but I don't remember any of our conversations. I do, however, remember the food. Pizza, subs, and Chick-fil-A nuggets are among some of the noteworthy meals we have consumed. Besides the eating, we play with the kids.

That's what dads like to do. The most memorable things about the playgroups I have had with Jason are all the times we have goofed around with the kids. I have learned a lot watching the way Jason interacts with his kids. If there was a scale measuring how concerned a parent gets over minor boo-boos, with a 10 being most concerned and 0 being unfazed, Jason would be a—5. Sure, he has compassion for his kids, but he also doesn't like the whining. Like most dads, he doesn't overly coddle the barely hurt, instead he focuses on getting his kids *back into the game*. Intentionally or not, Jason is a genius when it comes to redirecting a whiney kid back into play.

Like me, Jason enjoys watching kids have a good time. Since his kids could walk, they have had a supercool playground right inside their house to interact with. He literally turned their basement into a home version of Gymboree. There are mats of different sizes and designs and even a trampoline. When I hang out at his house, we spend much of our time watching the kids bounce, tumble, and genuinely enjoy themselves in the basement playground. We toss Nerf balls at the kids or ask them to do somersaults. We laugh when the kids fall down, and we encourage them to get back up and get back to playing. Most of all, we mediate.

When kids play together, they are undoubtedly going to have disputes. *She took my toy! He isn't sharing! She pushed me!* Exactly every ten seconds you can expect little kids to either hurt themselves or to have a dispute that requires parental intervention. It's best to moderate these situations properly early on; set the right precedent. There is no better training ground for both you and your kids than the playgroup setting. There are kids of varying ages and personalities interacting with each other. There are big girls and little boys. There are babies, toddlers, and elementary-school-aged kids on a holiday. Playgroups are a veritable tinderbox of childhood conflicts and one of the biggest ones is *sharing*.

Sharing Thoughts

What's the fatherly approach to sharing? First, it isn't a conflict until it gets out of control. Probably the best thing you can do as a dad is to ignore any initial disputes when sharing is concerned. Don't intercede unless you absolutely have to. It can be hard to do, but giving your kids the ability to work out problems on their own is very important.

Next, avoid stepping in and taking a toy from one kid who has just stolen it from someone else. If we step in right away and rip toys out of our kids' hands, we are simply teaching them to do the same. Let's look at an example replacing kids with adults.

Charlie walks into his office and looks around for his calculator. After opening and closing several drawers in his desk, Charlie decides to look in his coworker's desk. Charlie finds Marco's calculator, brings it to his desk, and begins to work with it. Marco enters the room and notices Charlie using his calculator.

"Charlie, is that my calculator?" Marco asks.

"Yes, it is."

On that, Marco stomps out of the room and quickly returns with their boss, Raymond. Raymond, upon seeing Charlie with Marco's calculator, stomps over to Charlie and rips the calculator out of his hands and gives it directly to Marco. Elated, Marco exclaims, "Yes!"

No one asked Charlie if he was almost done with the calculator. No one asked Charlie why he had the calculator in the first place. Now Charlie is super pissed, and the second that Raymond leaves the room, he takes the calculator back from Marco. A vicious cycle has been created.

If we give our kids a chance to work out their problems, they may just surprise you. Sure, give them guidance, but don't just react and snatch toys out of their hands right away.

Another great technique that I started employing in our house when Bella became a big sister was the **bait and switch**. **Bait and switch** is kind of like a Jedi mind trick for kindergartners that can be employed on toddlers and preschoolers. How does it work? In this example, we will use kids.

Bella enters the family room holding her favorite bear. She puts it down for a minute and starts to dance. Bella's younger sister, Mady, was in the family room to begin with and watched Bella put the bear down. The instant that Bella let go of the bear Mady picked it up and started playing with it. Upon seeing this, Bella runs over to me and says, "Daddy, Mady took my bear!"

"I know, Bella. Don't worry though, I have an idea. Here's what we are going to try. First, get another toy from your room that you like to play with. Come back down, and I will tell you what we we're going to do next," I tell her.

"OK, Daddy!" Instead of being mad, Bella is now kind of excited to be working with Daddy on getting her toy back. After a minute, Bella returns holding a doll, "Now what, Daddy?"

"OK, now just play with that toy and put it down. When you put it down, I bet you Mady will drop the bear, and you can get it back," I explain. "What do you think?"

"I'll try it," Bella says with a smile.

"Hey, Bella, high five," I put my hand up. Bella immediately gives me a big high five. I want to let her know that we are a team, and we are working together. After a minute or two of playing with the doll, Bella puts it down on the table. Like clockwork, Mady picks up the doll and drops the bear. Bella collects the bear up and runs over to me, "It worked, Daddy!"

"That's awesome, Bella! Good job!"

Bait and switch is all about problem solving. I taught Bella this technique when she was four and have since taught both Mady and Sophia. It doesn't work every time, but it does get kids thinking outside the box. It has helped Bella, and eventually Mady, start to create their own ways to solve problems. Sometimes their techniques are more primitive. Mady turned **bait and switch** into **go fetch**. **Go fetch** is basically a dumbed-down version of **bait and switch**. Mady would get a new toy, and instead of the subtle *watch-me-play-with-my-new-toy* maneuver, Mady would simply throw the new toy across the room and wait for the original toy to get put down.

Challenge yourself to come up with creative solutions. Talk to your kids, and get them to work together to fix the problems that face them. Modeling creative problem solving is a powerful thing as a parent.

Also, don't make everything about sharing. Sometimes kids aren't sharing because they are hungry, tired, bored, or all three put together. Sometimes kids aren't sharing because they are breaking molars or having an all-around bad day. Being a little kid is tough. Their bladders fill up at the blink of an eye. They have such a tough time trying to figure out the difference between the left and right shoes. They hurt themselves every day and are covered in new or worn Band-Aids. It's OK to give them a break on the sharing lecture and just move them from a toy setting to something different like coloring, dancing, or watching some TV. If your kids learn to share at home, they will be pros at playgroups. Nothing is more impressive at a playgroup than well-mannered and behaved children.

Dude, Use Your Words

Another thing to be on the lookout for during playgroups are physical confrontations. Toddlers and preschoolers act out by pushing, hitting, and biting. Why? It's a communication thing.

"D-d-d-ora!" A four-year-old girl sings as she enters the room carrying her Dora the Explorer doll.

"Mine!" A toddler boy exclaims, taking the toy away from the older girl.

Frustrated, the girl thinks for a second. *How do I communicate to this kid that I don't like what he did?* She isn't used to thinking so fast. She isn't ready to express herself on demand, especially in a stressful situation. The frustration mounts, and she quickly erupts by smacking the boy in the head. Sure, it was her fault, but what is the right reaction?

As a dad, it is really important to remember who we are talking to. We aren't disciplining our equals. We aren't addressing kids with even a year of education under their belts. For all intents and purposes, we are explaining civility to someone who has no concern for self-discipline. Toddlers and preschoolers are ***me-ists***. They want what they want, and they want it now. If you get in their way, they will get pissed. A little kid who is angry will use violence if you don't teach them why they shouldn't. They will kick, hit, shove, scratch, and bite. It really isn't their fault—they are ignorant.

Our job is to mold these little dudes into thoughtful members of society. One of the first big lessons is teaching our kids not to use violence as a way to communicate. We need to teach our kids to use their words instead of their fists.

"Hey, Mady, I know you wanted your Dora toy, but you need to *use your words*. Ask Max to give it back first, and if that doesn't work, find a grown-up to help you. We don't hit, OK?"

"OK, Dada," Mady replies.

Usually the younger kids are the ones who do most of the hitting and biting. Why? They get really frustrated being smaller, weaker, and slower. They are always a day late and a dollar short. No matter how hard they try, they can't be as fast as the older kids. They will always get the toys that the big kids passed on and, eventually, that gets old. Recognize that frustration. A good idea is to talk to the bigger kids at playgroups, and let them know that they need to look out for the younger kids. Encourage your own kids to look out for one another and to be aware of the fact that younger kids can get frustrated because they are little. This will only translate into public settings. The more they practice at home, the more they are able to take this show on the road.

Final Thoughts on Playgroups

Should you go to playgroups? Should you make the effort to enter this foreign culture? Of course you should. You should do it for you, but most of all, do it for the kids. Kids at a very young age learn from each other. Of course, there is a lot of parallel play going on, but learning to share toys with playmates is a lesson that should be taught over and over and as early as you can. Also, introducing children to other homes and their way of doing things is a lesson in itself.

Some houses have organic, vegetable-driven snack food, some houses have cookies and sweets, some houses have juice, some have milk. It is part of our job, in my opinion, to broaden our kids' horizons, and playgroups do that in a small way. Sights and sounds are different; the toys are different, but what remains the same is your presence. By remaining calm, reassuring, and smiling, we make it easier for our kids to transition from environment to environment. So go start or join a playgroup. Play with the kids, and talk to the parents—it's good for both you and your child.

<u>Walking into Parenthood</u>

"Sophia! Lunch is ready!" I called out to my youngest daughter. I thought to myself, *It's really cool watching my three girls grow up—I'm a lucky guy*. I had just finished making lunch, and it was time to corral Sophia to come to the table for a healthy PB&J lunch. "Sophia! Come here, sweetie!" I called again.

First, I heard a *little thud*. As a parent, you become accustomed to *thuds.* You can tell what they represent. A *heavy thud* could indicate injury or a broken artifact. A *medium thud* is the sound of kids on steps or just playing around. The *little thud* is the sound of a toddler hopping off the toilet or in this case—the couch. Sophia hopped off the couch in the family room with a *little thud*. Next, was the unmistakable sound of toddler feet quickly walking in my direction. As I made eye contact with her, Sophia said, "Hi, Dada!"

As I said, "Hi, Sophia," I noticed something wasn't quite right. Wait, what was all over her? What had she gotten into? *The gate was up, so she didn't go upstairs*, I thought to myself. As she walked closer, I saw she was carrying something in her hand—a *Sharpie*. She was covered in black permanent marker.

"Dada!" She smiled and jumped toward me unaware that I wasn't happy with what I saw. *How the hell did she get a Sharpie?* It only took me a few minutes to do the dishes and whip up a couple sandwiches. Sure, I had ESPN on while I worked in the kitchen, but how could she have gotten the marker?

"Sweetie, where did you get this?" I asked in my best, most patient voice. As she pointed in the direction of our cabinets, I quickly realized what had happened. Piecing it together, I realized that as I opened a kitchen drawer containing forks, knives and, yes, permanent markers, I had forgotten to rechildproof it as I continued to work in the kitchen.

Sophia, smart as toddlers come, saw that I was distracted by the TV and took advantage of a brief window of time and opened the coveted drawer and took the marker.

She looked ridiculous. Her face, covered in marker. Her body—torso to stomach—covered in marker. Her legs had scribbles all over the place. I started to wonder if she could be poisoned by the amount of marker ink she had used on herself. Then, I started to wonder what else she could have drawn on. That's when I saw the bench. I guess it's technically an ottoman, but whatever—I call it a bench. Cream colored, and apparently, the perfect palette for an eighteen-month-old wielding a *Sharpie*. I was humbled by the carnage she had created in less than five minutes. That day, Sophia taught me a lesson about parenting—*never* turn your back on a toddler unless you are sure they can't get the *Sharpies*.

When children start walking or doing a fast/aggressive crawl, the *real* parenting starts. Quickly, the peaceful, immobile baby that used to just lie around or swing in jumper swing all day is now invading your sanctuaries. Babies don't know the price tags associated with the items in their path. Babies couldn't care less how many payments have been made on a credit card to pay for the items in their debris field. Babies just want what they see—period. There is no rhyme or reason for what they want to get at, but basically, a good rule of thumb is that if a baby can get at it, they will want to get it, slobber on it, put it in their mouth for some period of time, and then drop it abruptly on the ground.

Early walkers are even more difficult because they are truly unreasonable. Our oldest, Bella, walked at nine months. Yeah, it's kind of braggy to be like, "She started walking at nine months," but when they walk that early, they are literally unstoppable. Early walkers want to do two things: break expensive electronics and bump their heads. If there are no electronics to get at, they will settle for bumping their heads on the corners of tables, the corners of walls, into cabinets, and on the ground. Our second child was much better; she walked at thirteen months. It was good because she was pretty stable when she walked, and she also respected boundaries a bit more.

Our youngest started walking at seven months. Looking back, I should have invested in a baby-sized football helmet. That kid seemed almost compelled to injure herself. Nothing severe ever happened, but neighbors probably thought I was beating her up or something. She always had the bruise or bump of the day. No matter how diligent you are with a seven-month-old walker, they will find a way to run into something.

Some of the time, it is really quite comical—babies are the only people I have ever seen who will walk right into a wall, fall down, and get back up and do it all over again. Their oversized heads must be difficult to control, and you can tell because they fall *melon first.* Like the way a cat always lands on its feet, babies seem to always land on their heads.

So what do parents do to limit the bumps, scrapes, and bruises while limiting the damages that babies can incur? Two things: *barricades* and *everything up.*

I really don't think parenting should be this huge "no" fest. Seriously, babies and toddlers don't really understand why they can't do something or why something would be off-limits anyway. I have seen some parents get frustrated because their baby or toddler just didn't listen when they *said* no, so they decided to *yell* no. No matter what tone you say no with, it just doesn't have a positive impact on the youngest of kids. So instead of throwing out *noes* ad nauseam, I recommend trying to find ways to adapt to your child's behavior. Remove temptation so you don't have to keep telling a ten-month-old or fifteen-month-old no over and over. It's better for both parties involved.

Barricades

Creating barricades is perhaps the manliest part of being a stay-at-home dad. It's kind of like creating an impenetrable fortress. The baby comes bounding over, tests the gate, finds out it's sound, and walks off in defeat. To me, babies are a lot like zombies. You know the movies where the survivors are frantically putting up loose boards to secure windows or propping dressers against a door? The zombies come up to the window, put their hands through the gaps, and test the planks of wood that stand in between them and a quick lunch. They tug, push, and rattle, making grunting noises—babies that is. Zombies moan and groan and walk off after testing the door that has a piano or some huge dresser behind it and walk off looking for another way in. I like to think of barricades along those lines; you are trying to keep the zombies out—but how?

Some barricades are store-bought, like outlet covers, baby gates, and cabinet latches. Some barricades, though, are homemade; these are the best kind. I have used tables turned on their sides, sofa cushions, bouncer seats, exersaucers (I am still unsure of the difference), chairs, love seats, bookshelves, rubber bands, twine, and practically anything that wasn't nailed down to help me keep my three daughters out of dangerous situations and out of our stuff. The only thing about homemade barricades is their durability. Babies never assume something is sturdy just by looking at it. They push, they pull, and they put their weight into trying to bring down the walls that separate them from expensive and breakable goods.

When you are barricading against both babies and toddlers, you need to think, "What would I do if I were a baby?" Or, "Where would I roll?" You need to outthink them, or they will get you!

Here are some steps to keep the zombies out:

Step 1—Outlet Covers

Zombies and babies hate outlet covers. They are way too clumsy to even attempt taking an outlet cover off. The outlet cover is about as confounding to a baby as calculus is to most adults. Keep it simple, and cover every outlet that is visible without exception. There is nothing worse than an exposed outlet for a baby. First, babies are attracted to them. Babies must think that outlets are toys built into the walls. I mean, they look like faces, and they are at baby level. No wonder babies go for them. Second, babies are covered in snot and slobber. A baby just standing in the vicinity of an exposed outlet is a shock just waiting to happen. It is estimated that roughly one thousand people die in the United States each year from electric shock, and with outlet covers sold at every grocery store, there is no reason that a baby should be in that figure.

Step 2—Gates

I think baby gates are great tools for keeping zombies out. Once secured, a baby gate isn't going anywhere. We have always had the tough, durable plastic baby gates. They are rugged, defiant, and just plain old intimidating. I think NASA should build the exterior of the future space shuttles out of baby-gate-ium. The height is enough to keep the babies off the stairs. Their rigid structure is enough to make babies only test them once a day.

For us, the most important place for us to secure has always been the stairs. Babies do need to figure out how to use stairs, but under supervision only. A baby going up or down the stairs alone is the equivalent of a drunk driver trying to navigate the Indy 500. Babies are clueless. They have no concept of "stepping down," and therefore, they simply tumble.

So where do I put baby gates besides stairs? Just like the zombie movies, you need to secure all vulnerable areas from the tots. For us, we had a gate keeping the kids out of the kitchen and the office. If this means buying three or four gates, do it. Peace of mind is more valuable than the cost of a fabricated baby gate.

Step 3—Cabinet Latches

Kitchen cabinets are accosted by babies and toddlers. They have some kind of crazy fascination with the allure of a closed door or a shut drawer. To them, no matter what's actually inside them, if it's in a cabinet or drawer, it is theirs and a toy. If you can't keep kids out of your kitchen via a baby gate, then you need to get some latches to keep the babies out of the cabinets and drawers that are within their reach.

Another great idea is to keep some of their toys in a kitchen cabinet or drawer so they can play while you work in the kitchen. You go to your space for pans and spices; they go to their space for rattles and stuffed animals—win-win. The biggest danger that drawers pose (besides what is in them) are pinched fingers. If a baby can hurt themselves—they will. So even if you have a drawer that a baby can have access to, make sure you keep an eye on them, or they will find a way to get injured.

Step 4—Homemade Barricades

At this point, the house is looking pretty good, but you are going to need to make sure that the DVD player doesn't get peanut butter inside it. You need to make sure vases don't get broken. You need to make sure your collection of Star Wars action figures don't get mistaken for toys and get played with.

Homemade barricades are all about two things: imagination and material. I suggest building some barricades to keep your wife out of your areas initially as practice.

"Hi, honey! I'm home!" your wife says as she shuts the front door behind her. "What the . . . ?" In front of her is where the entrance to the family room would usually be, but all she can see are sofa cushions stacked about six feet high. "Sweetie, what is all this about?"

"Oh, I am just trying to keep you out of the family room," you say nonchalantly.

"What? Why would you even *think* to do that?" she asks while walking toward the barricade.

"Well, you always try to get the remote control and put on the Lifetime channel. I figured I would stop all that," you say casually.

"The Lifetime Channel? Is that what this is all about? You know they have some shows that I bet you would like . . ." she says.

"La la la! I can't hear you! And no, they don't have shows I would like. You made me watch that one the other day. You said, 'You never watch anything with me.' I watched it and you know what—never again. That's why I put up this barricade," you explain yourself.

"Are you crying in there?" she asks.

"Maybe," you say with a whimper.

"OK, I promise no more Lifetime Channel, just take down these cushions." She pushes on the cushions that don't seem to move.

"Cushions!" you say laughing. "That isn't just cushions. I welded steel plates behind the cushions and propped the coffee table behind the steel plates. I'll see you when the game's over. Good night."

Now I am not recommending anything that severe. First, no one should ever have to watch the Lifetime Channel if they don't want to. Second, the coffee table was clearly overkill. Seriously though, homemade barricades begin with a curious baby and end with an imaginative caregiver. No matter what though, kids find a way to get through the defenses.

Evidence of My Barricading Failures

- Broken DVD player (poker chips inside)
- Baby carrying around tampons
- Baby wearing Q-tips in her ears
- Baby eating cat food
- Baby soaked from playing in toilet
- Baby flushing entire roll of toilet paper (separate incident)
- Broken TV (buttons pushed in by super strong baby)

My kids, I am convinced, try to embarrass me and usually perpetrate these crimes against me when a neighbor or family member is over. Nothing says, "You need to do a better job watching your kids," like a fourteen-month-old girl wearing her mom's panties over her head and carrying a tampon. So get a grip on the barricading thing, or the kids will make you look bad.

Some honorable mentions in the world of barricades are corner guards (you know, the rubber pieces you can put on sharp-edged tables to protect kids from cracking themselves), rubber bands (for securing multiple drawers) and, of course, duct tape.

Everything Up

Everything up is more of a philosophy than an actual methodology. I can't prescribe the best way to employ this technique in your household; only you know what will work best for you. When our oldest daughter, Isabella, started walking, I realized that babies and toddlers have a propensity to grab at everything in reach. We also found out that they are surprisingly strong.

We had one of those coffee tables with a pane of glass inserted in the middle. Any table in our house generally has at least one candle on it, and the bigger the table, the bigger the candle. I think Bella's first official act as a walking baby was to drop the big candle on the glass top of our coffee table. Thankfully, it didn't break, but the writing on the wall was clear enough; things had changed.

After that incident, we started looking at our rooms differently. What was dangerous and within reach? Up it went. Where is up exactly? Anywhere the grabby kid can't reach. We quickly became professionals in our house at identifying what needed to be moved out of reach and what didn't. This became true when we were out of the house too. The key is to remove the objects before the baby sees them; that way they can't miss them when they are gone. This requires sleight of hand. You must be swift and unseen like the wind. Both my wife and I became *everything-up* ninjas. At restaurants, you know they are going to go for the utensils, salt and pepper, sugar packets—so, like a cat, I pounce on those items and put them out of reach.

Visiting our parents' houses with our kids has always been fun. They have, of course, gone from being parents to becoming grandparents. During this metamorphosis, apparently, grandparents collect knickknacks—breakable, delicate little knickknacks and place them around the house in absolutely the most accessible areas for babies. It's almost like they are testing your parenting skills.

"Hey, hon, where should we put the shark jaw?" your dad asks your mom.

"Put it on the end table in the living room next to the crystal tea set and the two Precious Moments figurines," your mom replies.

"The angel figurines?" he asks.

"No, those aren't Precious Moments," she replies.

"Oh, so next to the plate we got from Austria?"

"Yeah, right there."

A grandparent's house can be like that. It's hard, but basically, each time you go anywhere, you need to be ever ready and thinking to yourself, *What should go up?* It will become automatic eventually. Just like driving a stick shift, it becomes second nature.

Besides trying to get at items that are eye level, toddlers are also taking aim at loftier goals. With the addition of climbing to their arsenal, toddlers will try to get into everything. Toddlers love to hurt themselves by climbing and subsequently falling off things. As toddlers learn to climb, you need to be on the lookout for the ultimate barricade failure—the prison break.

Escaping from the Crib

Operation Code-Named Climb out of the Crib, Land on my Head and Cry is what I like to call it. Toddlers want out of the crib, and they want it bad. They have no idea what they are going to do when they get out; they just want to do it. Toddlers learn very quickly. They learn to walk, talk, and go up and down steps so to them getting out of the crib is inevitable.

Getting out of the crib is like scaling Mount Everest to a toddler. Leaving stuffed animals in the crib is like leaving *Sherpas* to help lead the toddlers to the summit. They stack up plush toys, thus forming a primitive *base camp*. All eyes are focused on the ascent.

The crib should be an island. If you leave their cribs too close to dressers, curtains, or changing tables, you are just asking for trouble. Even if you take all the precautions you can, rest assured that one night you will hear a *heavy thud* come from the nursery. Once a toddler has reached the summit of Mount Crib, there is only one way to go—down. Toddlers are blessed with curiosity and, often, unwavering determination. But toddlers, like babies, are cursed with humungous heads. This is why 99 percent of these escapes end up failing.

Once a toddler has been able to scale the crib, they will keep doing it during nap times and at night. No one wants a toddler to bust their head falling out of the crib. So what do we do with the toddlers who aren't ready to be transitioned to the big-kid bed but are able to climb out of their crib? You may want to consider cosleeping. Safety is paramount. Stop the expeditions cold.

The Journey Begins

The journey of a parent begins when kids start to endanger themselves. You need to be vigilant. As a dad, you need to take pride in baby proofing the castle. You need to take a "not on my watch" stance when it comes to keeping the kids safe around the house and when you are out and about.

It may not seem like it, but you are setting an early parenting precedent with all that you are doing. You are making an extra effort to ensure your barricades are tight, which will in turn keep the "noes" to a minimum. The baby gate is a symbol in many ways.

We are putting up "baby gates" throughout our parenting careers. Maybe the baby gate is as simple as the choice of food we purchase for our kids or as abstract as the neighborhood we move into. As dads and moms, we want the best for our kids. We want them safe. We want them happy.

As a dad, we are telling our kids that we are prepared. We are telling our kids that we are there for them and that they will be safe. It's tough. It is the ultimate responsibility to care for someone so young and fragile. Of course, we are going to have our lapses—our mental breakdowns when a kid slides through our defenses. But being a dad means that we will be right there to pick our kids up when they fall down, dust them off, and make it all better.

Becoming Toddlers

Understanding toddlers is a huge part of becoming an experienced parent. What the heck is a *toddler* anyway? What makes a *toddler* different than a baby? What on earth is a *baby*? The most widely accepted definition of a *toddler* is a child who has begun walking. To me, that's doesn't always seem to fit. Some kids walk very early but are obviously just babies. I suppose both terms need to be defined so you know what you're dealing with as a parent.

What is a *baby*? A *baby* is a mammal creature that cannot hold cups. A baby is also typically marked by the inability to smell their own poop.

What is a *toddler*? A *toddler* is a mammal that can hold cups. A toddler can walk and generally speak a few words. Toddlers also begin to recognize smells emanating from their diapers. Toddlers are also marked by marginal coordination and a more defined personality. Toddlers are funny and always make noises like they are running downhill when they walk briskly. Compared to babies, toddlers are much more of a handful. They are defiant, dynamic, and have just enough physical prowess to be dangerous.

Rule of 50/50

A good friend of mine, John Harris, gave me a name for a universal toddler truth—*the rule of 50/50*. Even though you have a 50 percent chance of putting your shoes on correctly the first attempt, toddlers get it wrong nearly 95 percent of the time. Toddlers may in fact be **shoe dyslexic**. Shirts and pants also seem to cause toddlers a lot of problems. Toddlers are just trying to figure it all out. The shirt with the three holes seems almost impossible to them at first. *Which hole is for my head? Why is it so tight? I can't get my head through! I think I'm* *stuck. Let me try another hole. I'm stuck again! One more hole left . . . this has to be it. Phew! I can see again. Holy Teddy Grahams! This thing is on backward. I give up.*

Toddlers wear anything and everything backward. Shirts, shoes, pants, socks, coats, underwear, and even footed pajamas. I think because toddlers are so confused by clothes they simply abandon them all together and opt to go naked much of the time. Toddlers love nudity. It amuses them. Being *nakie* is about the pinnacle of the humor world for toddlers. They laugh at themselves, they laugh at their naked peers, and they laugh at their naked parents. Being naked to them is like this big party. It's like toddler casual Friday on steroids.

Being around toddlers all day can create a culture of absurdity that is hard to break away from. I remember one morning I wore my pants backward as I ran errands with Mady. I blamed it totally on being around toddlers too much. Jodi used to tiptoe around our toddlers in the morning when she was getting dressed. Many mornings she would dress in the dark just to allow the girls and me a little extra time to sleep. This all stopped when she went to work wearing two different shoes. Effectively we both know what it's like to be a toddler for a day.

Toddler Fashion

Toddlers have no clue about fashion. They go with their gut. Rain boots and shorts ten days in a row—Why not? I think toddlers should be allowed to express themselves. I am not saying that they should be allowed to go out in just their Skivvies. I just think that we shouldn't force them into our ideas of what fashion should or shouldn't be. To toddlers, braggable fashion choices are portions of Halloween costumes, brightly colored shirts, boots, and hats. Basically, toddlers would thrive at the Carnivale in Venice.

Don't fight the toddler's intrinsic need to embarrass themselves. After all, it won't be long before they will want the latest fashions and expensive clothes. Revel in the fact that they can be pacified wearing the same outfit for weeks at a time.

How Toddlers Get Around

Have you ever thought about how toddlers get around? They are hilarious to watch. I remember watching Sophia when she was two years old very clearly. I came to realize that she ran from place to place constantly. She would climb down from her chair after eating breakfast and run a full sprint into the family room to play or draw or whatever. Then, later, she'd put down the crayon or toy or what-have-you and sprint a reckless-kid-almost-falling-forward sprint into the living room to harass our cat until he couldn't take it anymore. Then she would run toward the family room again. She literally ran most of the time and almost never walked anywhere.

To put that in context, can you imagine running through your own house? How would that feel? How would it look? Toddlers don't think—they do. Of course, they run from place to place quite a bit, but there are other ways that a toddler can use to get from point A to point B. After studying toddlers for years, I have found that they really only move around in five different ways: *the sprint, the hop, the flip, the climb,* and *the mosey.*

The Sprint

This mode of transportation is used in 80 percent of all toddler travel. The sprint is used when a toddler wants to go anywhere and there isn't a slight step or incline or slight drop or object in front of them. *The sprint* is a toddler's loudest form of transportation except for *the fall.* A toddler running is the decibel equivalent of dropping a large book with each footfall. A toddler falling is the decibel equivalent of dropping two large books and usually is followed by a whiny sound. *The fall* is more of a form of stopping/braking for toddlers, but nonetheless, it is loud. *The sprint* is useful in tiring out toddlers. Toddlers don't realize that with each short burst of speed they are burning calories. They don't even know what calories are. They don't know why they are getting tired or why you put them on a treadmill.

The Hop

The hop is a utilitarian form of transport that toddlers use when they need to circumnavigate, dodge, or evade rough terrain. Rough terrain includes the last step in a staircase, small toys, pillows, leaves, *nothing,* curbs, books, and healthy food. *The hop* is an awkward form of transport and leads to many falls and is used only about 4 percent of the time.

The Flip

Once a toddler understands how to **flip** (a somersault) they will use this form of transport whenever they are around family or friends whom they would like to impress. Sure, **hopping** and **sprinting** are both impressive, but **flipping** is the preferred way for toddlers to show off. **Flipping** is also the essence of creative movement for any self-respecting toddler. If a toddler hears music that they enjoy, they will inevitably **flip** several times to show their approval. A **flipping toddler** is a toddler that thinks they are better than everyone else. Flipping is very rare and only happens 3 percent of the time.

The Mosey

The mosey is both a form of transport and a display of civil disobedience. Toddlers will mosey only when it is not desirable. Toddlers can show their utter disdain for the lack of chewy snacks or doughnuts or doughnut-shaped chewy snacks through **the mosey**. Although this form of transport is uncommon, it happens in direct proportion to the number of times that you anger your toddler.

The Climb

The climb is an extreme form of toddler travel. Toddlers use the climb to (A) get attention, or (B) hurt themselves. If a toddler recognizes that their parent is socializing with another parent for a period of time deemed unacceptable to the toddler (five to ten seconds), they will, without second thought, climb the most dangerous apparatus they can find. Toddlers also love to hurt themselves. The most foolproof way to accomplish this is by climbing something innocuous and letting go. The result is always a boo-boo worthy of showing every family member or friend for at least two days. Items toddlers climb contain, but are not limited to, siblings, chairs, animals, parents, toys, tables, stairs, toy chests, cribs, toilets, and anything that will collapse under small amounts of pressure and weight. While climbing is commonplace, it is thought that toddlers climb between 4 and 6 percent of the time.

Toddler's Gifts

There are other ways in which toddlers get around or, should I say, fail to get around that need to be included in this list. First and foremost is **the fall**. The fall is always funny. Toddlers always fall in ways that are ridiculous and look way worse than they actually are. Most toddler falls happen like this: egocentric toddler doesn't examine surroundings and walks into obstacle and falls down onto obstacle and begins to cry (see not hurt at all). Also, most falls happen within minutes before or after nap time.

The **abrupt stop** is a way in which toddlers are halted in their tracks from a sprint. The abrupt stop, like the fall, is always funny and happens like this: Toddler, who is busily looking at what they are carrying, runs head first into a wall or some other sturdy thing. This also *probably* doesn't hurt too much and is to be admired for its humorous attributes. When toddlers **fall** or come to an **abrupt stop,** they are doing so solely for our entertainment.

Toddler Language

Perhaps one of the biggest discerning characteristics of a toddler is how rapidly their vocabulary is developing. This isn't to say that toddlers are proficient at pronunciation, quite the opposite. Along with the explosion of words in your child's arsenal at this time, there will also be a sudden and steep increase in mispronounced/funny words. Some parents get really frustrated when their kids trip over certain words. I think this is a big mistake. A better way to approach the challenges that the English language presents is to document them. Here are some of my favorite mispronounced words that my daughters have used over the years and their definitions:

- **sumpin**—an unspecified object; the opposite of nuttin'
- **nuttin'**—having none
- **free**—the number after four
- **bemember**—not forgetting
- **owls-eye**—where playgrounds, trees, and beaches are; the opposite of ins-eye

- **sun scream**—sumpin we put on ourselves at the beach
- **baby soup**—an article of clothing we put on when swimming
- **waller**—we wash our hands with it, fish live in it, and we swim in it
- **ammal**—a creature that isn't a bug, fish, bird, or person
- **hair plane**—sumpin that flies in the sky
- **Sentruck**—a type of car made by Nissan
- **plig**—an animal that says *oink*
- **ins-eye**—where potties are; the opposite of owls-eye
- **baffroom**—where the potty is
- **flamily room**—where the TeeBee is
- **Tee Bee**—a box that plays cartoons
- **pinnano**—a musical instrument with keys
- **keekee**—a cat
- **froat**—where food goes down
- **toopays**—something we put on a *toobrush* before we brush our teeth
- **hock dog**—a red piece of meat that is served with cat-sup
- **peeza-deeya**—a toasted tortilla with melted cheese and chicken inside
- **banunana**—a yellow fruit
- **Yemen M's**—a candy chocolate with the letter *m* on them
- **pime-abble**—a type of fruit that is yellow; Spongebod's house
- **Spongebod Hair Cants**—a yellow, sponge cartoon character
- **Pliglet**—a cartoon pig and Winnie the Pooh's friend
- **Goofer**—a cartoon gopher and Winnie the Pooh's friend
- **fung**—not a finger; each person has two
- **nastics**—a class where we flip and jump

Embrace these times. Document them. Sure you want to start correcting your kids' mistakes along the way, but don't put too much pressure on them to be perfect. I say celebrate what defines them: how they talk, how they walk, how they can become so instantly defiant, and their logic.

Toddler Logic

On top of trying to figure out how to move their bodies, toddlers are also trying to get a handle on their minds. Like their bodies, a toddler's brain fails at an alarming rate. Mady, our middle child, said *last night* to represent any time before the present. For instance:

"Dada, d'you remember *last night* when it was snowing?" Mady asks as she wades in the pool.

"I remember, but that was a while ago, not *last night*," I tell her.

"Oh, I meaned *yesterday*," she corrects herself.

Life is very confusing to them. Sophia, our youngest, had an irrational fear of gumballs. No, I don't mean the candy you chew; I am talking about the seeds that fall off gumball trees. We call them *monkey balls*. One summer, I had to rake all the monkey balls out of our yard before she would set foot outside. She could spot them from the door.

Sophia was also convinced that *upstairs* was some kind of magical destination.

"Sophia, we need to get dressed before we go to the store," I said. "We need to go *upstairs*."

"*Upstairs?* Yay!" she said excitedly.

"C'mon, let's get moving."

"Dada?" Sophia asks in a bewildered tone.

"Yes, Sophia."

"Are we goin' *upstairs* at da store too?"

"No, just on the regular floor."

"But I want a go *upstairs*. Can I go *upstairs*?"

"We'll see."

"Yay!"

I had no idea what on earth *upstairs* could have possibly meant in her mind, but I am pretty sure she thought everything was better *upstairs*.

Sophia is also big into *thumbs-up*. When I see her doing something right or just being a good girl, I give her the *thumbs-up* sign. The only problem was that Sophia didn't ever say *thumb* exactly right. Instead of saying *thumbs*-up, Sophia would utter such gems as *fungs up, fung up* or, my favorite, *fucks up*!

"Dada, look at me!" Sophia hollered during her gymnastics class.

"I see you! Good job, Sophia."

Sophia made the thumbs-up sign, "Fucks up, Daddy!"

"Thumbs up, sweetie."

Toddlers try really hard to get it right. Sometimes it's OK to laugh at them because as dads we should be teaching them not to take themselves too seriously.

Toddlers are special, fragile creatures. The toddler years are trying times. They can be downright exhausting if you don't have the right outlook. So I challenge you to find the good side of your toddler. The side that makes you smile. The side of your toddler that is silly, uncoordinated, and wearing shoes on the wrong feet. Sure the terrible twos are coming, but we don't need to be dreading them. They can be a lot of fun.

Breaking the Toddler Horse

Life with toddlers is intense. For instance, a toddler under your care wants a yogurt; you open the fridge and see you are out of yogurt. You try to explain this to the toddler. The toddler doesn't care for your explanation. The toddler starts flipping out, and you are dead—or you just want to be.

A toddler could flip out for any number of reasons. It could happen because they got milk on their pants. It could happen because they didn't spill milk on their pants. It could happen because they knocked over some blocks. They could be flipping out because their fingers are sticky. Toddlers are picky, wild little creatures. They are just forming ideas of the world around them. Their morals: primitive. Their focus: me first. This is where parenting comes into play.

Explanations

One of the best ways to cut through the power struggles that develop between toddlers and their parents is to reason with them. Toddlers aren't as dumb as they look. Yeah, most of the time they are taking off their shirts and pants and spreading Oreo cookies all over themselves, but they are reasonable—to a degree. Instead of just saying, "Dude, no," to your toddler when they ask for something, explain to them why. For instance:

"Daddy, can I have that ball?" your son asks.

"Wow, that is a cool ball, but I need the money in my pocket to buy us food, and if I get the ball, we might starve to death. You don't want us to die, do you?" you reply. Well, maybe that's a bit heavy-handed, but you get the picture. Seriously, explaining things makes them feel more in control and that's a good thing.

Tell Them When They Get It Right

Being a stay-at-home dad isn't just about keeping the kids alive and keeping the house in order. Being a stay-at-home dad means that you are, well, a dad and that you are being parental. One of the most important things we can do as dads is to be that encouraging voice telling our kids, "Good work."

Toddlers are looking for praise and encouragement. "Did I do it right?" "Am I being a good kid?" Like a coach of an athletic team, dads need to be there to say, "Yes! Great job!" or, "Dude, you are being so good today!" We also need to be there when toddlers get it wrong and show them the *right way* to do it. We want to reinforce the good and acknowledge that we are watching—that we are proud.

Parenting Sleight of Hand or Finding Ways to Say Yes

Toddlers want everything. "Can I have five cookies? Can I play with the permanent markers? Can I watch that cartoon ten more times?" It's easy to say *no* constantly to toddlers. Let's face it; toddlers are super frustrating at times. But it's better to avoid getting caught up in their circular logic.

Example:

"Daddy, can I have that ball?" your son asks.

"Dude, no."

"But, Daddy, I want that ball," he replies.

"I said no."

"But I *really* want it!" he insists. You are getting nowhere.

Here's a better way to handle this example with ***parenting sleight of hand***:

"Daddy, can I have that ball?" your son asks.

"You know what's better than that ball?" you reply.

"What?" your son wonders.

"That really cool soccer ball at home," you say excitedly. "Can we play with it when we get home?"

"Yes," he replies. It's kind of like the Jedi mind trick, and toddlers fall for it *a lot*.

Sure, it's reasonable to say *no* as parents; but when kids are young, we should think, "How can I say yes?" It's challenging to think that way, but it pays off during toddlerhood.

What not to do

Your son, who is watching you paint your bathroom, asks, "Can I paint too, Daddy?"

"Absolutely not, go away!" you reply.

Finding a way to say yes

Your son, who is watching you paint your bathroom, asks, "Can I paint too, Daddy?"

"Absolutely! I need some help," you reply. "Let's go get you a brush, OK?"

"OK, Daddy! Yay! I can paint with Daddy!" Your son is overjoyed, and you are instantly a hero.

The more you make your *mini-me* feel like they are part of the process, you will find that they will become more confident, secure, and less likely to throw a tantrum.

Offering Choices

A great way for toddlers to feel in control is to offer them choices. Here are some examples:

"Would you like to have cereal or yogurt?"

"Would you like to wear the yellow shirt or the blue one?"

"Would you like to leave the park now or in five minutes?"

Just a couple options are enough. That will make them feel *empowered* and *important,* which is good. Don't offer too many choices because it can have a negative effect.

"Would you like cereal, toast, a bagel, waffles, oatmeal, a southwestern omelet, eggs Benedict, country fried steak, banana milk shake, french fries, or venison?" you ask.

"Toast."

"Whole grain, wheat, white, rye, pumpernickel, or sourdough?"

"Rye."

"Buttered?"

"Yes."

"Crust on?"

"No."

"Cut in half or in triangles?"

"Triangles."

Offering a toddler all those choices is dangerous. The last thing you want to do is give a toddler too much power. Toddlers who been given too much power have **Been Regalized At Toddlerhood (BRAT)**. A *brat* is marked by their constant demands and subservient parents. No one wants to see a *brat*—no one. The more power you give a *brat*, the more they will expect. Parents are supposed to be authoritarian, not the other way around. Kids look for discipline because it gives them order in their lives. Order gives them confidence. A confident toddler is better than a *brat* any day.

Toddler Discipline

Clearly, toddlers get less credit than they are owed. They are smart and getting smarter every day. That being said, you should be looking at the toddler years as the time to start employing early limits and regulations on your progeny. The key to being a good disciplinarian is **consistency** and **fairness**. Here are some key concepts to think about when beginning the early stages of disciplining your kids.

1-2-3 Magic

There is a great book for parents of power hungry toddlers called *1-2-3 Magic: Effective Discipline for Children 2-12* by Thomas Phelan. The concept is simple: set rules and outline consequences for those who are insolent. If a toddler is insolent, give them three seconds to be good. If they are foolish enough not to comply when you count to three—give them a time-out.

Time-Outs

The most common form of toddler discipline is the **time-out**. **Time-outs** are exactly what you are thinking . . . I hope. Basically, **time-outs** are like the penalty box in hockey. Instead of high sticking, there's running with scissors; instead of boarding, there's hitting. You decide what offenses are **time-outable.** It's your house—your rules. You may want to go as far as to have a time-out corner or chair (Plexiglas walls and door are optional) that they always have to reside in during a time-out, and you should seek to keep time-outs short. Using a timer is a good idea too.

An example time-out

"Dude, don't hit your sister," you say. Your son looks at you and looks back at his sister. "Dude—one, two," the sister gets smacked. "OK, that's it—*time-out*. Two minutes. You know you get two minutes for hitting." You hit the timer on the microwave. Congratulations, you are now a referee.

Understanding Toddlers

Toddlers are a lot like you and me. The main difference between toddlers and adults is how they react to adversity. What type of adversity could a toddler possibly have to deal with? There are two main sources of adversity for toddlers: hunger and exhaustion. Maybe that sounds familiar. I don't know about you, but I am at my absolute worst when I am overly hungry or really tired.

A tired or hungry toddler is a time bomb just waiting for a reason to blow. Anything can set them off. Simple requests, the most minor of injuries and sticky fingers can send a normally calm tot to self-destruct. Sure, sometimes those tears and tantrums are just a toddler demonstrating their will, but they could also just need a nap. They are growing like crazy; and the two ingredients that make growth possible, food and sleep, are also the elements that transform them into the temporarily insane. So the next time your toddler is acting up, you should ask yourself before you go straight into full **time-out mode**, *Are they hungry? Are they tired?*

One other important piece of the toddler puzzle is teething. Don't forget that toddlers start cutting molars when they are around two years old. Cutting a molar makes toddlers super pissed because it hurts. I suggest you stockpile children's Tylenol during this time frame.

Toddlers and Public Places

Toddlers and public places are a recipe for disaster. Toddlers pretty much love to assert their will whenever possible. If they are in a high chair or booster seat, they will want to get down. When they get down, they will want to be picked up. When you pick them up, they will want someone else to hold them. When someone else is holding them, they will want to be put down. Sometimes toddlers just want to run. Sometimes they want to yell. Sometimes they run into walls and cry. Every once in a while, you will see them grunting a bowel movement into their diaper. This is all well and good in the comfy confines of your house, but what about when you are out and about? Some places are great for toddlers, like parks and playgrounds. Some places, like church, are unavoidable. It is part of the circle of life to see a dad in the back of the church hanging out with his toddler. Some places though . . . aren't a good fit for toddlers.

Restaurants

We have all heard the baby crying in the restaurant. A baby is a baby; and it's understood that they cry, and generally, they can be soothed with a bottle or a walk with a parent. But toddlers? That's another story. Toddlers are beings of extremes. Toddlers scream when they aren't happy. They scream like the possessed during an exorcism. There is no *half-scream* with a toddler. It's always the full-blown, everyone-stop-what-you're-doing-and-look-at-my-kid scream. Now, why would a toddler scream in a restaurant? Because they want to get down. Because they dropped a crayon. Because you are taking too long to give them their sippy cup. Because they are hungry. I guess a better question would be this: Why wouldn't a toddler scream in a restaurant?

To a toddler, restaurants are very confusing places. There are all these smells. Food is everywhere. Strangers are giving them crayons, paper to draw on, and special seats to sit in. The problem with toddlers and restaurants is that toddlers don't get food as soon as they are buckled into their **eating seat**. Toddlers have been programmed to associate placement in their **eating seats** with the onset of food. Like Pavlov's dog, I theorize that toddlers start salivating and getting hungry when they see the **eating seats**.

There is usually a brief moment when the toddlers are captivated with scribbling on the paper in front of them, but that moment is fleeting. Soon, they are like, *I am so done with coloring. What's next? Wait . . . what the . . . . where's my food? This is an **eating seat**. This* *is a food table.* They get nervous. *Maybe it's not coming? Dada, I'm hungee! What did he say? Be patient! What the Huggies is he talking about? Patient? What does that even mean? Everyone else has food. Maybe they ate it all and there's none left! I'm gonna chew on this crayon. It tastes ok. Oh no! I dropped it! I need something to eat! I need to smack Dada and ask for food. Dada, I'm hungee! Huh? It's coming? But I don't see it. Is it invisible food? I hate this place. Time to scream. Wahhhh!* All this and you haven't even ordered yet.

If you are going to eat out with toddlers, go prepared. Bring snacks, sippy cups filled with juice, toys, books, and anything else you can think of to keep them occupied. Pay attention to them and focus on explaining what's going on around them. Also, restaurants are a great place for kids to learn to use their manners—set the right example, and show them how it should be. Also, don't be *those parents.* If you have reached the *point of no return* with your toddler, and there is absolutely no consoling them, be strong enough to leave. That's right, pay the bill, get the food *to-go*, and leave.

The Movies

First, babies and movies—don't do it. No one pays $10 for a ticket, $15 for popcorn, drink, and treats only to hear a baby crying or, worse yet, smell a nasty diaper while they chomp on Milk Duds. When you have a child, you have just said to the rest of the civilized world that you are now a movie renter. You are also saying that you will only go to the movies if you have landed a sitter. I have had movie experiences ruined, well maybe just marked by severe annoyance, because a couple just had to see *Kill Bill* or *Saving Private Ryan* and brought the baby along. If this isn't clear, a good rule of thumb is that if your child is in a stroller or carrier—*they shall not pass.*

Toddlers are only allowed to see kid movies—period. No exceptions. First, toddlers hate all other movies. Second, toddlers are restless. You can tell if a toddler is enjoying a movie by how quickly they want to run around in a theater. I think movie executives could learn a lot about the quality of their family movies by doing a test run first with toddlers only. If the toddlers get up within the first five minutes, they have just made a straight-to-DVD flick. If the toddlers last fifteen minutes, the movie isn't a classic—think *Madagascar 2.* If the toddlers remain seated for thirty minutes plus, you've got yourself a winner—most likely a Pixar film.

Toddlers also can only see matinees. A toddler watching a film at night is a risky proposition at best, and lest we forget, most toddlers are still pooping their pants. I remember the first movie we took each of our daughters to. Our oldest daughter, Bella, saw *Jungle Book II* as her first true theater experience, and she was fine. She sat through the entire movie without incident, granted, she was three at the time. Madeleine, born in 2002, saw *Polar Express* when it came out in 2004. She was a true toddler at two and half. I remember her yelling out at the start of the movie when snow started coming down on the big screen. Trying to say *snowflakes*, she yelled, "Noflakes!" Most of the theater heard her and laughed. It was one of the cutest moments ever. The rest of the movie was uneventful as far as outbursts, but she was truly captivated by the experience and lasted the duration.

Sophia's first movie was *Cars*. *Cars* came out in 2006, and she was born early in 2005, making her around fifteen months old when we decided to try and take her to the theater. She lasted almost forty-five minutes all told. I was shocked. We sat near the exit and went to a matinee, and it worked out fine.

So what are the rules for taking toddlers to the movies? Here are the toddler movie commandments:

1. Thou shall only take your toddler to matinees.
2. Thou shall only take your toddler to family movies.
3. Thou shall sit near the exit.
4. Thou shall remove your child if they are loud.
5. Thou shall remove your child if they have pooped their pants.
6. Thou shall remove your child if they are crying.
7. Thou shall not watch movies containing violence.
8. Thou shall not watch movies containing mature situations.
9. Thou shall not watch movies containing language.
10. Thou shall administer movies in the way of your choosing in the privacy of your own home.

Toddlerhood: Like that *Snap* It's Over

There is no going back. Once your kids have become toddlers, you will run into waves and phases of crazy behavior. People talk about the *terrible twos*. We always had more trouble with the *threes*. Each kid will bring a specific set of challenges. For us, Bella was overly sensitive, Mady had tremendous willpower, and Sophia . . . Sophia would finger-paint using the contents of her diaper.

She started her career in the dark arts when she was around a year and a half old after a particularly long nap. Usually, Sophia would start talking or whining to let me know she had woken up, but after this two-hour nap, she was still quiet. I decided to drop in on her. What I saw when I opened the door to her room still sends a shiver down my spine to this day. Sophia had taken off her shirt, pants, and diaper. She then used the contents of her diaper to create a ***fecal fresco*** on herself, the crib, and the wall behind the crib. Apparently, she pooped her pants before, during, or after her nap. At that point, she decided to take off her diaper and have at it.

This phase continued for months. It wasn't constant. Every few weeks or so, I was greeted with a fresh masterpiece. It was literally driving me mad. About the point when I was going to seek professional help for both my daughter and myself—it stopped. Looking back, it seems like it never happened. It was a passing phase. Toddlers go through phases. It's up to us to weather these phases and help our toddlers come through a particularly tough time in their developmental years unscathed.

Being a dad to a toddler is really all about setting the example. Don't lose your cool. Don't be a pushover. Be consistent, loving, and supportive.

The Preschooler Cometh

What's this? My toddler is losing baby fat and getting taller? They aren't taking naps all the time, and the whining is almost becoming manageable? Wait a second, you know what you've got there? You have yourself a **preschooler.** What's a **preschooler**?

Preschooler: A mammal human that is between three and four years old who is potty-trained. They learn very quickly and are developing both physically and mentally at an accelerated rate.

One of the biggest moments in any stay-at-home-parent's life is when their children are potty-trained. It's the equivalent of adding an extra hour to your day. Of course, having no more stinky diapers to change is huge, but you are also saving money on the transaction. You are **out of the shit**. Awesome.

Along with potty-training comes a whole host of other educational opportunities. The preschooler is a creature steeped in the "whys" of the world. Sure they will ask predictable questions. *Why is the sky blue? Why is the grass green?* Preschoolers aren't always pitching softballs though. Not too long ago, our youngest, confused about her vagina, asked me, "Daddy, do I have two butts?" Preschoolers ask some crazy things. *Where does the water go when we flush the potty? Where do cats go when they die? Is a burp when we fart out of our mouth? Why does blood come out when I fall down?*

Write their questions down and look up the answers together when you have time. Preschool is a golden time to be a dad. I have used the library, the Internet, and what I have learned through the years to answer all sorts of questions. Make sure your kids know that they can ask you questions and that you are resource they can tap into throughout their lives. The older your kids get, the more important it is to be seen as the "go-to guy" for answers.

During this time frame, kids will absorb limitless amounts of information. This is the time for educational movies, flash cards, and workbooks. Get their minds used to learning and the discipline behind learning.

Reading takes on more purpose at this time too. Teach kids to memorize the books you read to them at night. Let them finish the sentences that you start reading. Get early reader books that mesh pictures and words together. Work on the alphabet and letter sounds. Shapes, colors, and numbers are all fair game.

When you start educating your kids, you will realize that you have a huge responsibility on your hands. One of the biggest areas of debate is what we should name our body parts.

"Dada?" Sophia asks. We are in the middle of our morning routine. We are taking a shower together. It is just easier to take showers together in the morning, and toddlers know nothing about modesty.

"Yes, Sophia," I answer.

"Dada, what is that?" she asks as she points at *my package*. I had taken showers with Sophia since she was a baby, but it wasn't until she turned three that she asked me what the thing was hanging between my legs. I am a little caught off guard.

"Sophia, that's a penis."

"Oh," she replies. "Dada?" Sophia asked as she looks down at herself.

"Yes, Sophia?" I respond.

"Where's my penis?"

Should you call body parts goofy names like wee-wee, heinie, and who-who? Should we be up-front and tell the kids the anatomical names for our body parts? After all, words are just words. The truth is that it is us, the parents, who have a tougher time telling our kids the right name of our body parts.

"You don't have a penis, Sophia," I tell her.

"Is that my butt?" she asks, pointing below her belly.

I laugh, "No, Sophia—that's your vagina."

"Oh," she replies. "Dada?"

"Yes, Sophia?"

"Where's your vagina?" I am getting nowhere. After a short explanation about the differences between boys and girls, the lesson is over. Besides a blossoming intellect, toddlers are working on their physical capabilities. They are getting faster, stronger, and even more dexterous.

Preschoolers stop spilling their cups on a regular basis, which is a bonus. They can start playing Wii with some level of competency, and they are getting better at art. The preschooler is the most prolific creator of artwork. They are constantly coloring, painting, and drawing.

Throwing Away Children's Artwork

Drawings are truly how preschoolers express themselves. At first, their drawings are primitive. Scribble=person. Scribble=tree. Scribble=whatever they say it does. Scribbles are the first stage. The second stage of preschooler art is the stick figure. These poor stick figures start out with no hair, no feet, and no fingers. Overtime, their work once again progresses. The stick figure has hair, there are fingers, shoes, and the introduction of clothes—now we're getting somewhere. Still, the artwork is really crappy, and there's so much of it. All this bad art begs the question, "What should I throw away?"

The obvious answer is *all of it*, but that's easier said than done. Let's face it, kids are probably the most fantastic salesmen. We get these kids running over to us, out of breath, excited as can be, saying, "Daddy, Daddy! Look at this picture I made for **you**." You half expect to look down and see *Mona Lisa* eating at the *Last Supper* the way they're jumping around. Herein lies the problem.

This picture was made especially for **you**. It is special. They want **you** to have it. So you look at it and see perhaps a disturbing-looking creature with five heads that actually represents your family. The picture lacks basic construction, and the perspective is usually very random (it's a piece of crap).

The other part of the equation that is problematic is that your child wants your praise. You do a double take at the creature on the paper, and in your most sincere voice you say something like, "This is excellent . . . What is it?" Quickly, they go over the symbolism. They tell you what or who everything is. They spend twice as long explaining what they drew than how long it actually took them to slap the crude images haphazardly onto the poor piece of paper. With that, they disappear like a fart in the wind. That picture is now dead to them for all intents and purposes . . . until they find it in the trash.

Now if I kept every drawing/coloring my children ever did, I would be sifting around hip high in construction paper. This also sends the wrong message to kids in my mind. Should they think everything they've ever made is amazing? No. This gives them a false sense of confidence, and soon, this would lead to complacency in their technique. Before long, I would be getting crumpled Kleenexes and wet paper towels in place of drawings. I don't want that; I thought about it, and I think I deserve better. So I usually decide from a series of set criteria if the drawing or art project is **drawer worthy**.

You see, I have a nightstand drawer that is absolutely jam-packed full of kid artwork that my wife would stuff into the nearest trash can as fast as you can say, "*Sale at Ann Taylor*." I am more of a softy, so I am usually the one that rescues their art from abandonment. What are the characteristics I look for? What is my point system? How can I decide if something is **drawer worthy**?

How to Judge Kid Art

- Does the artwork contain at least one monster? 1 point per monster
- Does the artwork have a picture of Mike Wazowski from *Monsters, Inc.*? 1 point
- Does the artwork have one character from *Winnie the Pooh*? 1 point per character
- Does the artwork have random math? 2 points per random math problem
- Does the artwork contain a bean stalk? 1 point per bean stalk
- Does the artwork contain unfinished art? 1 point total (if more than 3 unfinished objects or characters, begin deducting points)
- Does the artwork contain unintentional profanity? 10 points per word (most important part of a child's art)

On this grading scale:

- **0 to 4** points: right in the trash
- **5 to 8** points: average—worthy of consideration
- **9 to 11** points: great work, immediately in the drawer

- **12 and over**: laminate now and put it in your fireproof box with your wills

Mady, now seven, drew something that embodied everything I look for in preschool art when she was four years old. What was Mady's drawing like? What did it score? The piece of art in question scored an astonishing 17 points! To this day, it hasn't been eclipsed. It even broke her old mark of 10 points tallied for her infamous "ass monster." See her artwork below.

The "Mady Shit" masterpiece

Remember, it isn't art because they said so; it's art because you said so.

Preschool

Probably the best thing about preschoolers is that they actually go to *preschool*. Preschool sessions only last around two hours, but that free time is a godsend. It is almost eerie having time for yourself. The house gets really quiet when you are alone. A couple hours alone will allow you to go to the grocery store unmolested. It can give you just enough time to mow the lawn. Two hours, though, goes by really quickly. It really isn't two hours after all. With the time driving and getting in and out of the car, you really only have an hour and a half. What can you do in an hour and a half anyway? It's basically a tease. But preschool isn't about us—it's about the kids.

Preschool opens up so many doors for kids. They learn with a group of their peers. They make new friends. They get to go on playdates and eventually to birthday parties. This new circle of friends is very much a part of the learning that your kids go through, but it is also part of the learning curve for you as the parent.

You will learn that almost every child a kid meets will be their best friend. Everyone is their best friend as long as they are in the same room with them for any period of time. The title of best friend is used liberally. So who will your kids see outside of school with so many best friends to choose from? That depends on you. You see, while the kids are inside the classroom making friends, you will be talking to the parents making new friends of your own. The kids whose parents you have most in common with are the ones that your kid will be playing with 95 percent of the time.

This leads us to the inevitable playdate. When you are watching someone else's kids, it is always interesting. It makes you wonder how your kids behave at their friend's house.

OPK

Maybe you remember the rap tune that had the refrain, "You down with *OPP*?" *OPK* is like that—sort of. It is similar in the sense that they are both acronyms, but the big difference is what they represent. *OPK* stands for *other people's kids*. You can look up *OPP* on your own time.

If you have ever watched someone else's kids, then you know what *OPK* is all about. I have watched *OPK* on several occasions, and I have made some notes regarding my experiences.

Poopies

If you ever have the misfortune to watch *OPK* who are still in diapers, you will come face-to-face with the *poopy paradox*. There are actually scientists who study this sort of thing. I actually knew what the **poopy paradox** was without having to pour stuff into beakers or having to get volunteers to fill out questionnaires. It's common sense. Basically, we start to adapt to the smell of our kids' poop. We form some kind of mild immunity to it. The introduction of some strange third-party poop will smell way worse because it's just different. The **poopy paradox** states that poop from **OPK** will smell about 500 percent worse than our own kids' even though they are both poop.

Food Consumption

I have found that **OPK** consume more food than mine. Granted, my kids don't eat a lot to begin with. Granted, I offer some of the finest chewy snacks and cut fruit around. No matter how good the food is, my kids always seem disinterested while **OPK** eat my food like it is their last meal.

OPK and My Cabinets

OPK open my cabinets on a ratio of 324:1 times more often than my kids do. This is a significant find and an absolute mathematical fact. I think that **OPK** are hoping to find some sort of Fruit Roll-Up land or a mythical toy depot behind one of my closed doors, but alas, they are more likely to find mismatched plastic containers and Brillo pads. **OPK** never seemed disillusioned in their quests to open, close, and reopen my cabinets. I am not positive, but I hypothesize that **OPK** suffer from a childlike form of Alzheimer's as they always seem surprised to see my adult hand closing the cabinets as they attempt to open them.

Behavior

This category can be separated into two distinct groups of **OPK**. The first group consists of **OPK** that are well behaved and or infants. This group regularly puts my kids to shame as they listen *and* use their manners. The second group, who I like to call *feral children*, seems like they jumped out of the pages of *Lord of the Flies* right into my family room. These *feral children* have distinct markings, which always include the following: disheveled or cowlicky hair, eyes that cannot focus on adults, and bumps on their foreheads. **Feral children** will run into walls, break my stuff, yell, cry, and basically piss me off.

Parents

Parents also fall into distinct categories. There are the parents that always say *thank-you* and offer to watch your kids in return and mean it, and then there are the parents that don't say *thank-you* and only offer to watch your kids as a way to blackmail you into watching theirs again (none of these kids are currently in my rotation). A rough day with **OPK** is acceptable and forgotten as soon as you get a sincere *thank-you*.

Not only is your child's peer group expanding as they enter preschool but so is yours. You will find that the older your kids get, the more friends you will make with other parents. The isolation that once plagued us as stay-at-home dads is beginning to fade, and we are quickly being accepted. I made my best friends during the preschool years of my children's lives. I am still close with many of the parents I met during this time. If you are going to a preschool and no one is talking to you, don't worry. It's not you—it's them.

As far as your preschooler goes, this is prime time to tell them how proud you are of them. Encouragement goes a long way. Don't expect preschoolers to get everything right the first time in class either. Having decent expectations is important as a parent, but it's even more important to prop your kids up when they fail.

Sex after Kids

The combination of sex and marriage is paradoxical. We get married to have sex, having sex leads to kids, and having kids leads to less sex. Sex after kids requires more work—plain and simple. Sometimes that work gets tiresome. When you get tired, you get lazy. If you are lazy, sex just won't happen. It is real easy for days to turn into weeks in between sexual encounters.

Before kids, sex was easy. It could happen at any moment. You could be eating breakfast with your wife and wink at her. The next thing you knew, you had just had sex! But this *spontaneous sex* is something that is way more difficult or practically nonexistent with kids.

Some people will go as far as to say that sex after kids is a myth. It's like the introduction of kids effectively neutralizes the libido.

"Honey . . . you want to cuddle?" your wife says.

"What's that supposed to mean?" you ask.

"You know what I mean," she says with a smirk.

"You understand we have a kid now," you tell her.

"Oh, that's right. Good night then," she replies.

It is ridiculous to accept defeat. Sure, there will be times when sex is almost impossible, but sex is a very important part of any marriage. A sexless marriage is one filled with tension and anxiety. Wives are thinking:

Does he still think I'm attractive?
Am I getting too fat for him?
Is it my hair?
Is it my breasts?
Guys on the other hand are thinking:
Is it my gas?

I told her I was horny, what more could she want?
Why is she always tired?
Why does she always have a headache?

Infants and Babies Hate Sex

Infants are notorious usurpers of time and attention. Infants, I also believe, can sense the exact moment when Mom and Dad are trying to get busy. They are crafty that way. They start crying, you start crying, and the moment is gone. A baby crying is like kryptonite to an erection. There is probably some science and math behind it, but the decibel and tone of a baby's cry is the most unromantic sound ever. The only good thing about trying to have sex when you have an infant is that they are immobile. I am sure if infants could, they would be knocking on your door to break up *sexy time*.

"Um, yeah, I know you're in there, and I know what you're thinking about doing," your infant would say if he or she could.

"Baby, I don't know what you are talking about," your wife pleads.

"Yeah, you do. And just to make sure you don't go through with it—I pooped my pants . . . Don't even make me cry," the infant says.

I think what is really behind an infant's ability to disrupt their parents is the fact that they don't want another brother or sister. Infants are very needy and don't want any competition.

Babies don't like parents having sex either. Babies have perfected the infant cry, and by this time, they have added something new to their repertoire—the scream. Babies can be very loud when they want to be, and it seems to happen at the most inopportune times.

As an organ, the penis is very fickle. It is afraid of crying infants and absolutely cowers when it hears a baby screaming. On top of all the distractions from the little children, sex becomes more difficult for another obvious reason—fatigue.

Fatigue assaults the most diligent dads out there. Adding a little baby to the family is difficult. There are the midnight feedings, the 3:00 AM diaper changes, and the 5:00 AM wake-up calls. It can wear on you. A week or two can go by very quickly when you feel like a zombie. All you can think about are the basic fundamentals: food, sleep, and shelter. *Sex? What's that?* Fatigue can also create problems in your romantic delivery. Instead of being subtle and going slow, sex becomes a utilitarian mission. You don't have time or energy to rub her back. You aren't picking up flowers from the store for her on the way home from work. Your gestures are short and to the point.

"How about some sex?" you ask your wife as you lie in bed staring at the ceiling.

"No thanks," she says plainly.

"OK, good night then," you reply.

"Good night."

You're tired, your wife is tired, and your moves are tired. You are in desperate need of some retraining. Here are some tips to consider if you want to have *more sex* with your wife.

Cleanliness Is Next to Sexiness

One of the most intense aphrodisiacs for moms is the sight and smell of a clean and orderly house. I heard about this one guy who couldn't expect to get any if the house was anything but spotless. Now, that is a bit much, but if you were able to surprise the wife with a spotless house, you may as well pencil yourself in for a romantic encounter each night the house remains clean.

Communication

I am not talking about communicating the fact that you want sex and you want it now, but rather, just plain old communication. Talk to your wife about her day, her interests, and maybe (I know it sounds strange), let her know that you love her. I am not talking an out of the blue, "I love you, sexy mama," even though that might not be a bad place to start. I am talking about sincerity. Tell her that she looks good, talk about her hair or her eyes. Basically, say and do all the things you used to do but have forgotten about through the years since the introduction of children.

Foreplay

Now, I know, most people think of foreplay as something that happens when sex isn't in question. I disagree. I think of foreplay between a couple married with children to be the little things like holding hands, hugging your wife, touching the curve of her back, massaging her shoulders—anything that is physical and not explicitly sexual. It's like if you have this car that has been sitting in the garage for a while—you don't just start racing it; you need to warm it up first. Think of it this way (in automobile terms): offer to brush her hair or rub her hands (kind of like starting the car), kiss her cheek or her neck (revving the engine), and for the win—holding her hips while you kiss her on the lips (peeling out of the driveway).

The Kids

Taking care of the kids is huge. Being a good dad is a turn-on for a lot of moms out there. There are many ways in which you can earn points as a dad that translate into redeemable points in the bedroom. Sex shouldn't ever be your motivation to be a good dad, but just keep in mind that the result can be rewarding in *many ways* (nudge, nudge, wink, wink).

Some Good Dad Ideas to Consider

Taking care of the midnight feedings: Nothing says I love you more than letting your spouse sleep while you take care of the kids. Not only are you being a good dad and bonding with your child, but you are also earning redeemable points with the wife. Win-win.

Taking the kids out of the house: Offer to take the kids out of the house by yourself. Let the little lady stay home to catch her breath. A wife who is overwhelmed and doesn't have time to relax once in a while is exponentially less likely to be in the mood. Take the kids out on a walk or to the grocery store. It really doesn't matter where you go; it's the thought that counts. Gestures like these are critical to ensuring your success later on.

Doing something educational with the kids: For babies, this could be as simple as playing peekaboo or talking to them as you carry them around the house. For toddlers, it could be reading them a book or showing them how to get dressed. For older kids, it could be helping with their homework or making a trip to the library.

Random Acts of Kindness

Being nice to your wife is always a good idea. If you *aren't* nice to her, then this list may be too advanced for you. If you *are* nice to your wife, pay attention to these ideas, and see how you can incorporate them into your daily routine.

Some Random Acts of Kindness to Consider

Going out of your way to pick up dinner from her favorite place or just making a nice meal: Food is a great way to get to a lady's heart. By acquiring or making food, you have already done something nice for your wife (especially if she generally makes the meals); and if the meal is something really savory, then you just got extra credit. Extra credit points are redeemable later.

Leaving love notes: A simple way to surprise your wife and have her smiling all day is to leave little notes around for her to find. The note could be something simple and sweet, "I don't tell you enough how amazing you are—I love you." That's a good *for instance*. The note could be funny and cute, "Nice butt!" is a solid example.

Being a gentleman: Treating your lady like a lady isn't chauvinistic; it is just a way of saying (through your actions) that you place your wife on a pedestal. Making your wife feel special is always a good thing—because she is special, right?

OK, so now you know what *to do* in order to have a better shot at getting lucky. What should we avoid though?

Things to Avoid If You Want to Have Sex

Don't Use Guilt

For some reason, guilt seems to be the default tactic men use to try and talk their wives into having sex. I believe there is a correlation between our horniness and IQs. As our urges increase, our IQs decrease at a flat rate. Because of this limited ability to reason, we say incredibly stupid things. For example:

"Remember when we didn't have kids?" you say to your wife as you lie in bed. "You were an animal back then!"

"What's that supposed to mean?" she says suspiciously. Sadly, this technique will get you less sex.

Don't Use Math

Never try to explain to your wife that sex should happen because it has been **x number of days** since your last encounter. That will only succeed in making your wife feel like she is being attacked. A wife under attack will fire back or run off and hide. Either way, your penis is pretty much locked down at that point. An example is this:

"According to the calendar, it has been a fortnight since we last made love, my dear," you say to your wife as you look at the calendar. "Shall we commence?"

No reply.

Einstein, this will only lead to another fortnight alone.

Don't Claim Sex with You Is a G*ift*

If it's your anniversary, don't give your wife redeemable love coupons. Sure, us guys wouldn't mind if our wives gave us those coupons, but your wife would rather have a day at the spa or a nice night on the town. Don't wrap yourself in a big bow and stretch out on the bed—you'll just embarrass yourself. An example of getting it wrong is this:

"Babe, I know the kids have been driving you crazy lately. So I got you something," you say, building the drama with a pause. "Sex with me!"

"You're kidding, right?" she asks in a serious tone. Why not get her something she will like better, like a single M&M's or Bran Flakes?

Don't Be Selfish

Being selfish in bed is always a bad idea. If you make it always about you, you may as well sleep in separate beds. For example:

Two seconds after starting to get *busy*, lovemaking is over. Your wife says, "Really? Is that it?"

"What, baby? Was that too intense?" you ask arrogantly.

"What about me?" she wonders aloud.

"What about you? I am going to bed," you reply.

Good luck with that one. Obviously, a dry spell will ensue if this ever happens.

Don't Be Boring

You need to be captain creative, not major yawn. The same thing over and over, while good at first, always gets dull overtime. Add variety and spice. This could mean setting up overnight trips and getting a hotel room on occasion. This could mean adding music to set the mood. This could mean dressing up in a costume—you know, whatever works for you.

Don't Strip for the Wife

Stripping for the wife is only to be done if you want her to laugh. Humor can be a turn-on, but if you're intending your dance to be provocative and exciting, you may be in for a surprise. There are a couple of reasons behind this. For one, you are most likely a bloated, less fit example of your former self after kids. For two, you may have never been in good shape, making your current state that much more humorous. Most likely, you aren't very flexible, and you look your best wearing a bulky sweater. Remember you are trying to get her *in* the mood, not scar her for life.

The truth of the matter is that sex begets sex. If you are sexually active, you tend to stay that way. If you go long periods of time without having sex, it is harder to get it when you want it. Why do these patterns happen? Men and women are different. Men have more of a physiological attachment to sex, whereas women tend to have more of an emotional connection. Because women have more of an emotional connection to sex, the more they get sex, the more they will want it. The same logic applies in reverse; if they don't get sex, they grow to have no emotional attachment to the deed—this is what you want to avoid.

So far, all we have talked about is what you should be looking out for if *you* want to improve your married sex life. *What about your wives? Are they exempt?* I don't think so, and they shouldn't either. I have compiled a self-help tutorial for wives who are trying to figure out how they can have more sex with their husbands. So if you are a guy reading up to this point—it may be a good idea to ***pass the book on to*** *your wife* to read at this time. Hopefully, you'll be thanking me when you get it back.

Things Wives Can Do to Have More Sex with their Husbands

Men are sensitive creatures. In many ways, men are immature and have trouble communicating what we want in a nonoffensive manner. Women, on the other hand, are expert communicators. If we are going to get sex after kids to work, it needs to be a total team effort. Guys will have to lean on the woman's strengths, perhaps her ability to communicate and plan. Women will have to lean on the man's strength—persistence. Seriously though, if you are interested in helping your sex life, read the following tips, and see how you can start implementing them.

No Nagging

Nothing makes a guy want to hit himself in the head with a brick more than nagging. Nagging is a serious turn-off. I am not sure why, but females seem to be genetically predisposed to being superior naggers. Perhaps there were ancient creatures that would die or run away if attacked by an adult female human wielding only a whiney voice. We can only guess at this point, but what is clear is that women nag. I am not a math guy, but I would venture to guess that as *nagging decreases*—quality *sex increases*. If you want to have better, more frequent sex, think about easing off the nagging or nixing it completely.

Initiate

Men aren't machines, and after years of marriage and children, it becomes difficult for them to play the "game" all the time. The game in question is the one that revolves around the unspoken tradition that the man has to initiate *the magic*; otherwise, nothing will happen. It is fine, say 80-85 percent of the time, for us guys to initiate things, but if the women in our lives would take over every once in a while—it would go a long way. Us husbands would feel better about ourselves, and this would certainly help spice things up.

Communicate

Ladies, although you may think your man is a mind reader—it simply isn't the case. If you want us to know what you want (in the bedroom), you are going to have to tell us. We would love to know what you are thinking because we really have no clue. Talking can only lead to a closer connection between you and your husband, and that is one thing husbands and wives both want.

Keeping Up Appearances

If you want to have better sex with your husband, then it isn't a bad idea to put your best foot forward. A lot of guys say things like these:

"She used to try harder to look good for me when we first got married."

Or maybe, "She always looks so nice when she goes to work or when she goes out with her friends—why doesn't she try to look good for me?"

Ladies, sometimes your man needs to be reminded just how beautiful you are. I am not saying that you should wear lingerie all the time or that you need to apply ten layers of makeup every hour. I am talking about making an effort to look sexy for your husband every once in a while. We'll even let this count as you initiating. It may be tough for you to part with the raggedy T-shirts and baggy sweats, but give it a try every once in a while and see where it gets you.

Promises

If you talk/schedule/hint/think about having sex one morning or afternoon, just keep this in mind—we will never forget. Your husband is about one million times more likely to remember what you say about sex than just about anything else. Like elephants, we remember.

Don't forget. If we need to remind you what we had talked about earlier in the day, the sex has already begun to suffer. If we remind you and you say something like, "Oh, well, I have to get to bed." Or "I have a headache—not now," you may as well pencil in a grumpy-guy guilt trip. It hurts our feelings. It makes us feel unimportant. Holding up your end of the bargain is crucial. One of our biggest thrills as husbands is to be lucky enough to be in our wives company intimately, and we take those discussions about future plans of romance to heart.

Fun

Sex is not work; it is fun. If you treat the act as an obligatory gesture—your husband can tell, and this will lead to a lower self-image for your husband and friction in your marriage. Have fun; enjoy yourself. There isn't a bigger turn-off than uninspired sex. If you have been guilty of treating sex as work in the past—resolve not to do this in the future as it will only lead to greater conflict down the road.

So there you have it. Sex is a very important part of a healthy marriage, and your sex life isn't something you should neglect. A happy marriage is a strong marriage. A strong marriage has a big impact on your family. In other words, having a good sex life will trickle down and positively affect your household in general. If you like what you just read—keep reading.

Wives, you may now **return the book to your husband**, or buy another copy for yourself.

If your wife just returned the book and she is rolling her eyes—my bad. If she's returning the book and is giving you *the look*—you're welcome. Seriously though, a strong marriage is integral to raising a family. The importance of an active, healthy sex life in a marriage shouldn't be overlooked. While I am not advocating that our lives need to be controlled by our sexual urges, or lack thereof, I am suggesting that sex does play a role in our relationships. How much sex should I be having? Well, that's completely up to what is best for you as a couple. Some couples are fine with the occasional encounter. Other couples would prefer to have sex more frequently. There is no right or wrong answer to determining the right amount of sex you should be having in your marriage.

Mastering the Art of the Quickie

Everything speeds up after kids. The weeks go by like days. It can be hard just to find the time to talk to your wife about her day. Meals are prepared and eaten quickly. TV programs are TiVo'd and fast-forwarded through. Patience is a commodity. How do a busy mom and dad manage to find time for sex amid the chaos of the *daily grind*? Through mastering the *art of the quickie,* any couple can make time for sex.

Quickies or quick sexual encounters aren't all about fast sex. A quickie starts with a *change in attitude* toward sex in general. Quicker is better. Quicker is more realistic. Quicker is reality. Don't take it from me; some eggheads actually discovered that sex is best when it is between three to thirteen minutes long.

Talk about Quickies

Where to begin? Make sure this is something that you talk to your wife about. Don't expect her to be a mind reader. After she's on board with this new philosophy toward sex, you need to set the mood. It's all about preheating the oven. A quickie at 5:45 PM starts with you smacking her butt in the morning in the bathroom. It begins when you give her a steamy kiss right before she drives off for the day. Ingredients can include sexy text messages and e-mails or a note that you put in her coat pocket.

Now to the logistics—how can we make this happen? First, never assume anything with kids. Don't assume they are asleep. Don't assume they aren't right outside your door listening. Don't assume that one of them isn't under your bed hiding.

Don't Get Caught!

I am sure there are worse things than a kid walking in on their parents having sex, like World War III for instance, but it's not a long list. Let me be clear about this: if you are having sex—**lock your doors or theirs**. Maybe even go as far as to prop something up against your door like a bookshelf or an armoire. You don't need distractions.

Next, pick the **proper venue**. The venue depends on two factors: time of day and if the kids are asleep. If it's two in the morning and the kids are asleep, you can get your quickie almost anywhere in the house. Being creative with the venue is a good thing too. The bedroom is so predictable, and near the cat box is bad.

It could be more planned like in the bathroom. I mean, the shower is logical. The sound of the running water drowns out whining kids and whatever noises the two of you are making. It could also be as simple as face-to-face in the laundry room. Just think, "Do we have three minutes to spare?"

Quickies might not be pretty. You might fall over trying to get your pants off. You might head-butt your wife in the middle or step on her feet, but a quickie isn't supposed to be perfect. What a quickie lacks for in planning, pomp, and circumstance, it makes up for in passion and spontaneity. And sometimes aren't passion and spontaneity exactly what a marriage needs to reenergize it? Think about it.

Date Night

I know I just finished talking to you about the importance of quickies, but married couples also benefit from taking some time to enjoy each other's company. Enter *date night*. Date nights are planned evenings out for married couples.

Sure, this sounds like a great idea on paper, but there are some common mistakes that can be made by the novices to the *date night* culture. Perhaps the biggest mistake that can be made for a couple on a date night is to assume that you will have something to talk about.

"This is a great place," your wife says as you enter the restaurant. "Great job picking it out."

"Thanks. I thought you might like it," you reply. "I'll tell them that we're here."

After talking to the hostess, you return to stand next to your wife in the lobby. The next few minutes drag by in silence. You can't help but notice happy patrons laughing at the bar and having what appear to be the most interesting conversations ever. You look at your wife and smile; she smiles back. You keep trying to think of something to say, but words fail you. Finally, you say something terrifically bland like, "It was a nice day today." *Did you just talk about the weather?* What is going on here?

Are We Boring?

It isn't that the two of you are boring. You are just out of your element. You aren't used to being around adults. You are used to a kid tossing carrot puree across the room. You are used to dinner accompanied by you or your wife making the sound of a *choo-choo train.* You are used to having kids dominate your attention. When you have time to have a quiet thought, you realize that there aren't any thoughts up there. It happens a lot.

A good bit of advice is to keep up on current events. Talk about politics and what is happening in the world. Jodi and I have had some riveting conversations about *nationalized health care* and *local government* during date nights. Also, remember that you used to talk about your dreams and aspirations before kids entered the picture—never stop dreaming. Talk about the kids too. Sure you are trying to get away from the kids for a night, but that shouldn't mean it is taboo to talk about the little hellions.

All that being said, initially, it may seem harder to pass the time with your wife when you are out on a date. You aren't used to having your wife's undivided attention. Usually you are competing with kids, pets, work, and TV. When *date night* is infrequent, it can seem awkward that it's just the two of you *alone*.

Plan Accordingly

If you haven't been out together in a while, plan a night out around an activity. Going to the movies is a great icebreaker. Pick a movie that you are both really interested in seeing and plan dinner afterward. You will go into dinner already having something to talk about. The activity is only limited by what you like to do. Maybe you want to go see a local concert, get a dance lesson, or take in a play. Maybe you want to go out to a karaoke bar. Whatever it is, you will leave having lots to talk about.

Bring Friends Along

Double date, triple date, or go out with a group of friends. Sometimes it's great to go out with a group of friends and enjoy not only your wife's company, but also the company of other adults.

Be Mindful

I have found that my ability to tolerate alcohol has diminished with each child we have had. Worse than that, the hangovers are more severe. I am not an every day, week, or month drinker, mind you; but sometimes just a few beers on a night out will result in a surprise hangover that lasts most of the following day. Also, if you drink too much on *date night,* you will have either (A) bad sex later on that night, or (B) no sex later on that night. Either way, be mindful—drink in moderation.

Date nights are about reconnecting. As a couple, we look forward to date nights. We love being nostalgic, and we love thinking about what the future holds. If *quickie* is the equivalent of giving the *marital battery* a hot shot, *date night* is like buying a completely new one. My suggestion is to make date nights special and as frequent as your schedule and budget will allow.

This Used to Be Our House

A house that is lived in by a family is very different than a house that is lived in by a couple. Everything in a house is assaulted when you raise children. In the process of writing this book, my daughters have ripped down blinds, squished blackberries into our carpet, broken multiple dishes, drawn on multiple tables, and scribbled graffiti on virtually every wall in their rooms. That's what I can remember. That's what I have discovered.

Our house that once was the pinnacle in design, comfort, and character has become a banged up, beaten-down version of its former self. The walls are all marked by handprints. The **handprint line** has grown with each passing year, becoming a visible reminder of the fact that our little girls are only getting bigger.

Sophia and Our Walls

The walls are dingy, marked up by the occasional misfired toy or shoe that was indiscriminately kicked off. The walls are drawn on with crayon, pen, pencil, and magic marker. Around the time that Sophia stopped smearing poop on the walls is around the time that she developed a keenness for other mediums.

When she was almost two, Sophia started hiding markers in her diapers. I wasn't prepared for Sophia in many ways. Bella was about as close to perfect as a kid could be. As a tot, Bella was smart, obedient, and fun to be around. Mady has always been quieter than Bella. She was a little headstrong at times and, once in a while, was prone to random acts of destruction; but overall, she was very, very good. Sophia, compared to her sisters, was a tornado. She is about as funny as a kid can be, and at the same time, she is cunning, dexterous, and underhanded. Sophia would make a great pickpocket. Instead of trying to make money though, Sophia has focused her talents on dismantling our house one room at a time.

Her room is testament to her love of drawing and her love of stealing markers, pens, and pencils when you aren't looking. At a certain point in time, I stopped painting over the drawings. There was no point. What Sophia liked to do in her room, she loved to do in her sisters' rooms and throughout our house. Eventually we convinced her through threatening her existence to stop drawing out in the open.

Mady's Messes

When we first moved into the house that we live in today, everything was new. The house smelled like paint and freshly installed carpet. It was a palette for us to create a home. We loved our house then, and we still love it to this day. We all christened the house in our own ways. I remember Jodi stained the counter in our bathroom somehow. Shortly after that, I spilled pencil shavings on the carpet in our room. Bella chipped a piece of the counter off in our kitchen. Then there was Mady. When we first moved into our new house, Mady and I spent the days together alone. Bella was in kindergarten, and Sophia wasn't born yet.

One day when I was home with Mady, I had fed her lunch and went upstairs to do some cleaning and unpacking. Mady was approaching three and was acting more and more like a *big girl* every day. I trusted her to eat her lunch. There was even a TV in the kitchen for her to watch. After five or ten minutes, I came down to check on Mady to see how she was doing with her lunch and to bring her up to help me with the rest of the chores. As I came down the steps, I saw Mady spring up from in between the living room and dining room. She ran off to the kitchen. *What the . . .*

"Mady, you're supposed to be eating lunch," I said calmly. "What are you doing?"

No response. Mady is famous for not answering questions. I walked over to the area right between the two rooms where she had been when I came down the stairs. That's when I saw a box of Swiss Miss Hot Chocolate torn open and twelve packets ripped and poured out onto the carpet. Mady had christened our new house with cocoa powder and marshmallows. She even poured milk on the pile of powder for good measure.

Now I'm not sure if you have ever tried to clean up cocoa powder and mini marshmallows with a vacuum. I am here to tell you that it doesn't work. I swear I can still smell chocolate in those rooms.

Mount Saint Mady lay dormant for over a year. I thought her career was over and that making messes had stopped. I was wrong. I remember it was a typical weekday home with Sophia and Mady. Sophia was almost two and Mady was four. Mady had finished her lunch and wanted to go upstairs to play. I lifted her over the baby gate and returned to the kitchen to clean up some dishes and make sure Sophia finished her food. Sophia picked at her food like a baby bird just learning how to use its beak. Sophia, a talker, also kept asking me questions the way typical toddlers do.

"Dada, whatcha doin'?" Sophia asked.

"I am doing the dishes, sweetheart," I answered.

"Whatcha doin' the dishes for?"

"Because they are dirty."

"Dada . . ."

"Yes, Sophia?"

"Dada, my hands are messy."

"Just eat, Sophia, I'll wash them when you're done."

"OK, Dada. You're a funny Dada!" She laughed.

Sophia has a way of relentlessly getting and keeping your attention. After I was done with the dishes and done with Sophia's parade of nonsense, which equated to a conversation, I realized I hadn't heard anything from Mady. Silence is never good when the kids are awake. Silence means they are either plotting something bad or in the act of doing something bad. Either way, you can pretty much assume the worst. The silence normally wouldn't have gone unnoticed any other day, but Sophia was extra vigilant with her questions that afternoon. Sophia was actually an accomplice in my mind to what Mady was perpetrating. Her job was to distract me so that Mady could get into whatever she wanted. Sophia was setting a *parenting pick*.

A *parenting pick* is when one child distracts a parental unit long enough to allow another child the opportunity to destroy a portion of the house without interruption.

I started to wonder to myself, *What is Mady doing?* I called to Mady, "Mady! What you doin' up there?"

Mady's response was the sound of her feet running from her room to the bathroom followed by her yelling back, "Nothing!"

Nothing, my ass! I said to myself. I knew something was up. I quickly made way for the stairs, hurdled the gate, and ran up them. "Mady, what are you doing?" I asked again.

"Dada, I'm sorry!" She started crying.

You know something really bad has happened when the first real response you get from your child is *I'm sorry.* The tears weren't a good omen either. *What the hell did she get into?* I wondered. As I reached the top of the stairs, I started to smell something. It was a pleasant but strong odor. *Coconut? Why the hell am I smelling coconut?* I made for her bedroom, and the smell intensified. That's when I saw it. In five minutes of time alone, Mady had taken a full bottle of shampoo from the bathroom and emptied it. She emptied it in her room on the carpet. In haste, when she realized she had screwed up, she attempted to cover the mess with a towel. It was a futile attempt. The towel was lumpy in the middle and the smell was a dead giveaway.

"Mady! Is that shampoo?" I was super pissed.

She stood there motionless, afraid to speak or move. Tears were streaming down her face.

"Mady! Why did you do this?" I tried a different way. I was just trying to figure out why she would have thought to empty shampoo on the carpet.

She shrugged her shoulders.

I felt bad for her, but the gravity of this crime was deserving of more than just a time-out. Mady's punishment was to help me pick up the shampoo mess. Most of it came up with a towel, but a rather significant amount remained in the carpet. Mady and I tried to use a bucket of water and rags to get the rest of the shampoo out of the carpet—no dice. After about forty-five minutes, we accepted defeat. Mady had worked off her crime to my satisfaction, and I couldn't keep going. There was no way the shampoo was going to come out, and we had multiple buckets of suds to prove it. The mess was colossal—almost humbling. I eventually opted to let the shampoo dry into the carpet. It was soap after all—how could it hurt?

The shampoo managed to rear its coconut head over a year later when we were getting our carpets steam cleaned by professionals. I remember the *technicians* calling me upstairs and asking what had happened in a certain section of carpet. I knew right away what they were talking about. Apparently, they were having a tough time getting an area to *stop foaming*. I am glad to say that Mady never poured shampoo on our carpet ever again.

Besides Mady's cocoa and coconut attacks, our carpets have seen it all. Grape juice, marker, mustard, peanut butter, and gum are some of the heavy hitters. Sure there's dirt, leaves, grass, and the like—that's a given. I suppose one of the worst messes we have ever had in our house was the time that Sophia got into Vaseline.

Sophia at Home with Mom

I like to think that I am a good dad and that I keep a pretty vigilant eye on my kids. Every once in a while, Jodi reminds me that I do a pretty damn good job. Sure she tells me, but sometimes, it's what the kids do when she is watching them that speak of my parenting skills. There have been significant disasters that have happened when the girls are under the watchful eye of my wife. Typically, Jodi doesn't get a lot of time alone with just her and the girls. So if you were to average it out, there is a much higher chance of something getting destroyed when the girls are with her than with me and that makes me smile. It makes me smile because I feel like I am doing something right. Sophia has written on three major pieces of furniture with magic markers—one of them under my watch. Sophia has gotten into lip gloss and smeared it all over the place a few times on Jodi's watch. Her most notable mess though is the time when Sophia got into the Vaseline.

I remember coming home when the girls were hanging out with Mom for the day. They were busily doing laundry together, but as I made my rounds kissing everyone hello, I noticed Sophia was absent. "Where's Sophia?" I asked.

"I don't know. I think she went to the bathroom," Jodi answered. That's when we heard little feet come down the stairs and make way toward the family room where we were talking. As Sophia turned the corner, we noticed a sort of *shimmer*. "Sophia!" Jodi exclaimed. "What's all over you?" As it turned out, not only had Sophia gotten Vaseline all over herself, but she had also smeared it over all the knobs on all the drawers in every room upstairs. There was Vaseline all over the TV in Bella's room. There was Vaseline all over one of the chairs that Sophia had drawn on with magic marker.

"Jodi, were you watching her?" I asked.

"Joe, I swear, she was only upstairs for a few minutes," Jodi replied desperately.

"Jodi—I know," I told her. "Now you know what I have to deal with every day. She's relentless."

"I see that," she answered.

So what can you do when your kids are constantly trying to wreck your house? Fight the good fight, or accept your place in life. The *lived in* feeling that your house portrays is normal and to be expected.

Document the Disasters

Accept the messes. Don't expect your kids to be perfect. It's OK if they make a gigantic mess every once in a while—it's what we sign up for when we decide to have kids in the first place. As a dad, it is important to document the messes. Take pictures for the photo album. Roll movies and capture the events forever on film. The epic messes are very frustrating in the present but something we look back on as parents and smile about later. Sometimes that fatherly perspective is needed when messes are made. We need to find the humor in the situation. One thing my dad taught me is to always look for the humor in tense situations and effectively diffuse them. What's the better lesson to be teaching: that we need to be perfect when we are three, four, or five years old; or that sometimes messes happen and that together we can make it all better? It's OK to be angry, but it's even better to be cleaning up the mess with your kid, turn to them and smile, saying, "What were you thinking?"

Evolution of Housework

OK, now that your house has been destroyed by your kids—it's time to clean. Cleaning comes in two forms: the *quick clean* and the *real clean*. Before kids, it is very likely that your home was much easier to maintain; but since the rug rats have entered the picture, you will notice that chores aren't the same. With your energy level getting zapped from all the chores, errands, and diaper changing, it is quite likely that you have begun to feel more and more comfortable with a house that revolves around the ideology of the *quick clean*.

Not only will you make your peace with the idea, but you will also get good at the *quick clean*. You will be like a *quick-clean ninja.* Your body will get used to the repetitive nature of stuffing books and toys in drawers and baskets. You will start to achieve muscle memory for the perfect amount of force needed to toss a cushion onto a couch from several feet away. You will become Michael Jordan with stuffed animals. You will know exactly where the priority messes are and just how long it will take to pick them up. Your mind could shut off completely and still your house would somehow be relatively clean in thirty minutes. All of this *quick cleaning* will lead to you feeling detached from the ivory tower notion of the *real clean*.

Sure, the *quick clean* is a facade, but an effective one. A *quick clean* consists of making sure everything is in its place and the kitchen is clean. You will do things like shuffle pillows on beds and couches, put toys and books away, put dishes in the dishwasher, and sweep up larger messes. No vacuuming, dusting, or mopping is required. This facade can only continue for so long though. The stickiness of the floor, the dirt in the carpet, and general nastiness that abounds will speak to your body of work.

Because you are a guy, chances are you are competitive. So it stands to reason you will begin to reach critical mass with a dirty house as it affects your sense of pride. Once this happens, you will achieve the **real clean**. The **real clean** only happens when the conditions are ideal. Like the *perfect storm*—everything has to be just so. You will need time, desire, the right tools, and fuel.

The Laundry

As far as I am concerned, the mother of all chores is the laundry. The laundry is a metaphor for anything relentless. No matter how many times you do the laundry, there is more waiting just around the corner. If you think about the laundry too much, it will drive you crazy. Who makes laundry? Babies make laundry—lots and lots of laundry. It is all dirty and most of it smells like formula. The smell of formula, after some exposure to it, begins to achieve the effect of triggering a wicked gag reflex. The formula smell is the smell that you pray for though. The **other** smells that radiate through baby laundry take on a life of their own. What is worse than the smells? Folding the laundry of course. Folding little tiny laundry is absurd. What is the point really? I mean the onesies can be wrinkled, right?

If babies are the gifted and talented of the laundry creation world, toddlers are virtuosos. Toddlers make laundry almost instantly. Toddlers wipe absolutely everything on themselves. Whether it is a toddler wiping a sticky finger on their pant leg, or a toddler wiping their nose/mouth with their sleeve, you will quickly see that toddlers *never* stop making laundry. Toddlers, late in toddlerhood, discover that they can change their outfits. As soon as the *outfit-changing floodgates* open, it is nearly impossible to close them. Instead of having heaps of nasty baby laundry, you will now have heaps of toddler laundry. Toddler laundry ranges from nasty undies to perfectly clean shirts that were put in the hamper alongside the nasty undies. After a piece of laundry reaches the hamper—it gets washed. Think of it this way: you wouldn't eat a clean piece of fruit if it was sitting next to the cat box, would you?

Putting laundry away seems like such an afterthought. It is kind of anticlimatic. You have washed it. You have dried it. You have folded it. Isn't all that enough? I think I hate putting laundry away most of all.

The Dishes

The dishes aren't quite as bad as the laundry, but they can be every bit as gross. Dishes come in all shapes and sizes. Doing the dishes could mean putting an empty formula bottle in the dishwasher, or it could mean cleaning off the high chair. High chairs are areas of great concern. Toddlers simply wipe stuff on themselves—babies wipe stuff indiscriminately. Babies wiggle, squirm, and shuffle in their seats. With each twist and turn, the average baby can deposit as much as five tablespoons (based on no reliable data) of debris in or on their high chair or seat. This debris may start out as *cream of rice,* but invariably, it will end up as *cement.* As an aside, if for some reason we ever ran out of whatever is used to make up cement, I am quite sure I could come up with a great substitute.

Toddlers, although slightly more dexterous, create more dish-related problems than babies. Toddlers, because they are slightly more dexterous, achieve **top-off** status with their drinks at some point. **Top-off** status is highly sought after and always precarious. A toddler can have **top-off** status one day, and the next, it can be revoked. **Top-off** status is a privilege like a driver's license. Let's say your toddler recently has been awarded **top-off** status, and they have no accidents for a week or maybe two weeks—everything is going well. *Right?* Wrong. Week three hits and they dump chocolate milk on themselves. You shake it off and give them another go at it. Orange juice later in the week has betrayed them. You go to the well one more time—grape juice is now the culprit. You institute martial law. All drinks must have lids again until your sanity returns. **Top-off** status has brought you extra laundry and more time with the mop in one week than you spend with your wife in a month.

Dishes are more of a frame of mind than an actual chore. There are ways to conserve dishes. For instance, napkins make great plates. Another great tip is to use the same cup over and over, day in and day out. Simply rinse with hot soapy water and that cup is ready to get back in the action. Try to think of how to eliminate dishes—you aren't being lazy; you are being creative.

Getting Kids Involved

Who can do chores? To be able to do chores, you need to be able to walk and understand the difference between what is clean and what is dirty. There is no reason not to involve kids in the cleaning process from an early age. The great thing about kids as opposed to teenagers is the fact that they blindly like to help. *Daddy, what are you doing? Can I help?*

It isn't unheard of to involve two-year-olds with household chores. The more kids you have, the more labor you have. I think if I had a couple thousand kids, I could build a decent-sized pyramid, but that's neither here nor there. The point is—don't hesitate to start assigning responsibility to your kids.

What Kids Can Do

Here is a list of reasonable chores that your kids can start helping with around the house.

A two-year-old can

- take off dirty clothes and put them in or near the hamper,
- take off clean clothes and put them in the hamper next to or on top of soiled clothes,
- pick up small amounts of toys without becoming overwhelmed,
- put cushions on couches,
- put books away,
- put leaves and yard messes in bags,
- pick up their room with help,*
- put plate on table.**

*Tip: I suggest sitting in the middle of their room with them and direct them how to pick up. The more you teach them to do, the more they will be able to do in the future *on their own*.

**Tip: At this age, I suggest creating an area in the kitchen that is reachable and accessible for them and only keep their bowls, plates, cups, and utensils there. They will be happy to get their dishes out and set them at their place on the table.

A three-year-old can

- reasonably make a toddler bed,
- align shoes in their closet correctly,

- put dirty dish in the sink (as long as they can reach),
- help with laundry matching socks and basic folding,
- brush their teeth and wash their hair,
- water plants,
- clean up their own small spills,*
- set themselves up with small snacks.**

*Tip: At this age, you can set your kids up with their own cleaning supplies. I am not talking hazardous chemicals here, but a spray bottle filled with water and paper towels. These items should be accessible in the kitchen, so they can pick up their own messes.

**Tip: At this age, think about buying drink boxes and keep them in a lower shelf or even a drawer in the refrigerator. Have a drawer or bin that is accessible in the kitchen area that contains healthy snacks. Get them used to doing things for themselves, and gradually, introduce them to more responsibilities as they get older.

A four-year-old can

- help with basic meals,
- help load and unload the dishwasher,
- wipe off counters and tables,
- dust,
- pull weeds out of gardens,
- use a dustpan and brush.*

*Tip: Keep a dustpan and brush in an accessible location for your kids.

In general, you should aim to keep chores something that your kids want to be involved in. If you assign them a chore, and it's clear they can't do it, the result is a kid that feels helpless and unimportant. The last thing you want is a workforce that suffers from bad morale. You want a team that knows their role and is able to perform.

Also, **don't pay them**. This will set a bad precedent of *quid pro quo*. Kids need to understand the value of contributing to the greater good of the family instead of helping out just to get some extra pocket change. On top of that, most kids have no clue how much money is worth anyway. For example, here is a conversation I had with my four-year-old Sophia about money:

"How much money do you think Momma makes in one day?" I asked her.

"Umm, seven," she replied.

"Seven what? Seven dollars? Seven cents?"

"Umm, seven dollars *and* seven cents."

"OK. Well, how much money do you think Momma makes in a year?"

"Ten thousand coins."

"How much money do you think a box of cereal costs?"

"Hmmm, eight coins and eight credit cards."

"OK, what do you want to be when you grow up?" I asked.

"A basketball player . . . a soccer player," Sophia replied.

"A basketball player and a soccer player?"

"A soccer player," Sophia corrected me.

"How much money do you think a soccer player makes in a year?" I asked.

"Ten thousand dollars," she answered definitely.

"So what is more, a *coin* or a *dollar*?" I asked her.

"A coin."

"A coin is worth more money?"

"Yep."

Paying toddlers and preschoolers to pitch in is ludicrous. It makes just as much sense to light your money on fire. Teaching them that you value their help is what's important here.

Trust, but Verify

So the kids are going to help with the chores. Tidying their room and helping in the kitchen and with the laundry are all pretty standard ways in which kids can help around the house. Be warned though, the biggest mistake you can make with kids is to let them clean and not check their work. Sure, we trust them, but we need to make sure they are following through.

We were lulled into a false sense of security with chores with our first daughter, Bella. When I asked her to help—she helped. When I asked her to pick up her room—she did it. I checked behind her initially, but it was obvious that she had a built in moral compass that kept her true to her word. Then came Mady. Mady thinks outside of the box. She is into art. She loves animals. She could spend hours picking berries from our garden in our backyard. She builds tremendous forts out of our sofa cushions, and she loves to find ways to skirt her chores.

When Mady turned six, we expected her to pick up her room on her own. We expected it to get done because Bella always listened. Of course, I still checked to see if her room was clean when she said it was, but the problem was, it always appeared clean. Mady's room actually looked cleaner than Bella's from a superficial, cursory glance. The bed was made, the stuffed animals were lined up, the drawers shut, and her dresser was nice and tidy.

One day I made a startling discovery though. I went in her room to find a pair of socks. She was complaining that she couldn't find any. Socks seem to vanish in our house. I buy them by the gross in huge twenty-four-count packs, but they still seem to evaporate into thin air. So, already a bit frustrated, I started searching in Mady's sock drawer. As I looked in her drawer, I noticed something behind her dresser. Behind her dresser were not only socks, but panties, dresses, stuffed animals, pants, shirts, toys, and crumpled-up pieces of paper. Like a magician pulling on a never-ending thread, I started taking everything out from behind the dresser—it just kept coming.

Reaching down to the very back of her dresser, I grabbed up the last of it. That's when I noticed what was under her bed. The amount of clothes and toys was absolutely staggering. I was enthralled. I pulled everything out. I found a pair of my own shoes that I couldn't find for weeks. I found some of Jodi's clothes. There were lots of Bella's and Sophia's outfits. Moldy bath towels. Blankets. Sweaters. Coats. Boots. The pile of stuff that Mady had been hiding instead of putting away was mounting. That's when the thought came to me—*the closet!*

I opened the closet and was greeted by a mountain of unfolded clean and dirty clothes. Up to this point, I was stunned and emotionless. When I opened the closet though, I came to grips with the fact that I was beside myself pissed. "Mady!" I yelled.

Mady came rushing into her room. She saw the pile I had made. She saw me staring wildly into her closet. She looked up at me and said, "You got me." *You got me*. She knew that she was hiding things. She knew it was wrong, yet she still did it, but why? She did it because she could. I wasn't checking her work closely enough—lesson learned. Trust, but verify.

The most important thing with chores is to make them part of your culture. Introduce chores to your kids early. Teach them how to help.

Teach them the value of a job well done. Encourage them to think of themselves as capable instead of helpless. Our goal as dads and parents should be to train our kids to do things on their own.

Remember, chores have no gender. There is nothing feminine about folding the laundry or washing dishes. You can introduce your kids to both the routine household chores and those that are generally reserved for men. Let your kids help shovel the snow, take out the trash, and lend a hand with yard work. Dads today are constantly breaking down barriers. When our sons and daughters see us iron a shirt or put clothes in the dryer, we are teaching them that our roles aren't defined by society—they are defined by the individual. These lessons are learned through osmosis and go beyond many of the traditional things we think of as parenting.

Dads Teaching While They Play

My dad worked a lot of swing shift when I was growing up. What did that mean for us as a family? There were times when we had to be really quiet during the day so he could get his sleep. There were times when he was grouchy because of the toll the hours took on his system. Those details were just minor players in the bigger picture of what swing shift meant. Swing shift meant that my dad was home during the prime playtime hours of the day.

I remember my dad teaching my brother and I how to play Wiffleball in the cul-de-sac where we grew up. My dad was a teacher and mediator for all the neighborhood kids. In that paved field of dreams, my dad taught us more than how to play a game; he taught us how to get excited about life in general. He loved it when anyone got a hit. He would razz us when we struck out, and he was always patient enough to give the younger kids four, five, and even six strikes. Manhole covers and mailboxes served as bases. The curb at the far end of the court was the fence and an automatic homerun. We were using our imaginations to create our own make-believe stadium, and it was all because of my dad.

My dad was laying the foundation for who I was to become. With each witty jibe and each word of encouragement, my dad was equipping me with all the necessary tools to mentor my friends and, eventually, my children. It wasn't always Wiffleball; my dad taught us football, baseball and, especially, Ping-Pong. Most of all, my dad taught me social graces and how to interact with people through humor and humility.

I think it's important to respect our kids enough to teach them at their level—through play. Passively, through play, my dad taught me so many of life's lessons, and that's the power of what it means to be a dad. You can teach your kids just through goofing off. Kids need to learn from playing, using their imaginations, and even falling down. That's what dads bring to the table.

So I encourage you to play with your kids. Build forts together out of sofa cushions. Play Wiffleball. Make up your own game. The more you play with your kids, the more you will teach them about civility, competition, sportsmanship, and about yourself.

For my part, my dad inspired me to coach. I coach chess, outdoor and indoor soccer, and basketball. I have been a basketball coach to our oldest daughter since she was old enough to hold a ball. We have a video of her first Christmas playing with a toy basketball hoop. It stood all of three feet tall, and she made her very first basket. Over six years later, when Bella made her first basket in competition, I was her coach. When the ball went in the hoop, I flipped out. I remember picking Bella up and carrying her down the court to play defense. I was so excited, and I didn't care what anyone else thought. It's my job to tell my daughters how proud they make me. It's my job to inspire them. It's my job to teach them not to take life so seriously and how to be humble and kind. My dad taught me that with a Wiffle ball and a plastic bat when I was five.

Surviving More than One Kid

Having more than one kid leads to culture shift as a parent. What began as the pursuit of perfection often just turns into *survival*. One kid means diapers, tantrums, messes, and less sleep. Now multiply one child times two, three, or even four. Get the picture? A great metaphor for what it's like having more than one child is the simple act of getting your kids into the car.

Getting the Kids into the Car: Operation Code-Named Fifteen Minutes of Hell

Here's the scenario: you are a parent trying to get your kids out the door. You are rushing around trying to get out the door on time. You are getting frustrated because the kids aren't cooperating, thus, making your job harder.

Finally, you get them ready and start collecting yourself. You get your keys. You put your coat on. All the pieces of the puzzle are in place, and you're about to walk out the door. That's when you realize one of your kids isn't there. You call out their name. No response. You call them a second time and then a third, and just as you are about to lose it, they appear.

The *laggy* child appears, but in the two seconds it took you to get your coat on and find the keys, this child has undone your best-laid plans. They stand before you completely disrobed. They will have none of your deadlines and urgency.

Tip: In these situations, it is really easy to flip out and go completely berserk, and although that is a solid option, I would actually recommend laughter.

Your child's random act of sabotage has just cost you valuable time. You will now be late for wherever you are going (see who cares). You have officially been initiated into a sad club, a club I would like to call the *Late by Association Club* (LAC).

Late by Association

This phrase represents a group of parents who, after having more than one kid, have found it difficult to arrive on time to many events. They are constantly being sabotaged by their own children, making it nearly impossible to get anywhere expediently. Acts of sabotage include, but are not limited to, the removal of shoes, socks, all clothing, pooping their pants, getting dressed incorrectly (mismatched, inside out, seasonally wrong, or backward), taking out ponytails, spilling a drink on themselves, and putting on Halloween costumes.

Perhaps the most notorious saboteur in our family is Mady. Mady, our middle child, has shoe issues. She is always losing her own shoes or hiding her sisters' shoes. When Mady was six, she performed her greatest act of sabotage. We were getting ready to leave for Bella's basketball practice. I was the coach, and we not only had to be on time, we needed to be there early. Bella was hysterically looking for her shoes. She had been looking for them for forty-five minutes. Bella never misplaces things—it just didn't seem right that she would lose her shoes.

"Bella! Where are your shoes?" I yelled.

"I don't know!" she answered. "They were in my closet. I don't know where they are." Her voice was frantic because she knew I was getting super pissed.

"Where have you looked?" I asked her.

"I looked in my room. I looked in Sophia's room and Mady's room. They're not in the hallway or downstairs," she answered. "I don't know where they are, Daddy." Whenever my girls say *daddy* instead of *dada,* they are in full self-preservation mode. We had five minutes left to look for the shoes before I absolutely had to leave. We started tearing apart all the places where toys go. We looked under beds, in clothes drawers, and even in my closet. The shoes weren't anywhere.

"OK, you just won't practice, Bella. Get some other shoes on," I told her. I am sure my face was flushed. How could an entire family search a house for fifty minutes and not find a pair of shoes?

"Oh," Mady said, "Bella's shoes?" *What's that? Did Mady know where they were?*

I watched in amazement as Mady climbed behind the entertainment center in our family room. It was a place where only Sophia, our cat, and Mady could fit. When she emerged from the depths, she was holding Bella's shoes in the air. I had no time to flip out on Mady. We had to get to practice. I was actually in shock. I was in shock that Mady hid Bella's shoes intentionally. I was in shock because she waited so long to actually get them. But I was mostly in shock because of Mady's demeanor. She had just witnessed her dad tear apart the entire house. She had listened while her dad barked at her big sister for answers to why the shoes were missing in the first place. She acted like it was no big deal.

"Here you go, Dada." Mady passed me Bella's shoes.

I was defeated. My blood pressure started to return to normal levels. "Get in the car," I said in my normal-dad voice.

I have come to notice that I am not the only parent in the **LAC**. I have also noticed that club members have sympathy for those other parents who run late on occasion. Perfect parents who are never late for anything generally scorn late parents. They roll their eyes and whisper to each other. These parents actually belong to their own club. The **Always Scorning Someone** club or **ASS** club is very annoying and probably the reason why **LAC** members rush around so much in the first place. If you ask me, I would rather be *late by association* than an *ass* any day of the week—but that's just me.

Sure, there are times when we have to be somewhere at a specific time, and it can get stressful trying to orchestrate an entire family. There are also times when having more than one kid can create some major logistical problems. Shopping, for instance, can go very smoothly or can be an absolute disaster.

Shopping with Kid(s): The Incident

As parents, there are many times that our interests, needs, and even our health are put on the back burner as we tend to our kids.

Although this is true, there are some times when nature will wait for no one, not even a whiney brat.

Something horrible happened to me once when I was out on a shopping trip with my two youngest daughters. I was shopping in the heart of *Bel Air*, a nearby town. I liked shopping there because it has Target, Kohls, *and* Toys "R" Us, making it a great place to go to cross off multiple items on a shopping list.

We had eaten fast food that day and were bouncing through the stores at a frantic pace, which always makes my belly ache. I had no time to pay attention to the rumblings in my tummy and continued along at a torrid clip, grabbing up diapers, socks, birthday party presents, and the inevitable DVD for the kids faster than you could say *Imodium AD*. The more I tried to ignore my stomach, the angrier it became.

Up to this point in my life, I had always been a world-class suppressor. I could hold back natural urges almost at will like it was some kind of superpower. I was confident my stomach would settle once again like it always had in the past. I was flaunting my invulnerability at God like those who claimed the *Titanic* was *unsinkable,* and well, we all remember what happened there.

Just when I had finished a trip to the last store on my list, my bowels started to quake. As I strapped my offspring into their seats, I came to the realization that I was going to need to drive home in record time if I wanted to utilize the *home throne*.

After I had tied in my daughters and sat in the vehicle, reality hit. *I wasn't going to make it home.* Maybe it was the act of sitting or the pushing on the pedals, but no matter what had sped up the timetable, it was clear that the *home throne* was a fool's dream. My house in *Havre de Grace* was around fifteen to twenty minutes away, and my date with destiny was a fraction of that. As I started to pull out of the parking lot, I shifted from trying to make my way to the interstate to trying to find a bathroom. If I didn't find a bathroom soon, I would most certainly be driving home in soiled cargo shorts. *Damn you, McDonalds!*

Then, out of the clear, strip-malled blue sky, I saw it—Barnes and Noble. It was like seeing a porcelain oasis after walking miles in a foreign city devoid of restrooms.

"I've always liked *their* bathrooms," I thought to myself. I had to act fast. I was getting cold sweats, and my kids were locked in tight to their safety seats. Each movement I made was amplified somehow. I was more keenly aware of my surroundings at that moment than any other moment in my life. The sound of my blinker sounded obscenely loud. The car seat seemed rough and unforgiving. The lights on the dashboard were blinding. I heard the tires rub against the pavement as we turned into the Barnes and Noble parking lot. We had made it.

I expertly slid my minivan into an uncomfortably tight spot (the only thing available ever at our Barnes and Noble) and quickly engaged the vehicle in park and jumped out of my seat in one fluid motion. Getting the girls out of the car never took so long. The sound of belt buckles unsnapping resonated in my bowels. The way Mady slowly sauntered out of the minivan made it seem like time itself had stopped. I noticed french fries on the floor, hair clips, stupid fast food toys, and miscellaneous wrappers. I was about to explode, and Mady was moseying.

Finally, we escaped the minivan. I grabbed up Sophia and began to pull Mady across the parking lot. I calculated how far the entrance was and how far I had to go from there to reach the ivory tower, which was a Barnes and Noble's clean restroom. *This is going to be close.*

I pushed through the doors into the store. It was very bright inside. It felt like I was being *reborn*. My eyes quickly adjusted. I saw a store filled with customers. I heard the murmur of conversations and transactions. I had a strange sensation of being paranoid. Maybe it was the desperation in my eyes, or the fact that I was running in a direct line toward the bathroom, but I couldn't help but think that everyone in the store was looking at me. It felt like they all knew I wasn't a paying customer. It felt like they could read my mind. They knew I was about to *light up* the bathroom.

I thought for an instant that severe diarrhea perhaps brought some kind of extrasensory powers. I got the feeling that I was somehow transformed and enlightened by the deluge being held back by my impossibly strong sphincter.

I had to focus. The light at the end of the tunnel was just ahead. Everything was coming to a climax. Passers-by even parted, noticing the urgency and determination on my face. Mady asked, "Dada, why are we running?" I couldn't think. No time to answer. I only had time to plow past the men's room door.

Entering the bathroom, my eyes instantly found the handicap stall. I needed the wide berth with my daughters in tow. It was empty!

I will spare you the details, but that day changed me. Having one of your most mind-numbingly forceful bowel movements with a toddler on your lap and a five-year-old staring at you gives you a feeling of empowerment. It was as if I was initiated into an elite corp. I feel if you can go to the bathroom with a toddler on your lap, you can accomplish anything in this world.

The Experienced Parent

After years on the job and weathering more than one kid in diapers, you will begin transitioning from the *rookie parent* to the *experienced parent*. What is an *experienced parent*?

Experienced parent: A parent who rolls with the punches and understands that sometimes life with children doesn't always go as scripted. *Experienced parents* don't care about public perception. *Experienced parents* don't care about superclean houses. *Experienced parents* are cynical and tough. If an *experienced parent* and a ninja were to fight, the world would have one less ninja by fight's end.

You can tell *experienced parents* from *rookie parents* just from their body language. They are more relaxed. They react less quickly to the sounds of crying kids. They know how to motivate their kids into obedience with just a look. The *experienced parent* has faced adversity and has lived to talk about it. Battle tested, nothing surprises them. It is where we are heading and where some of us already are.

As *experienced parents,* we can cut through the BS. Sometimes we go out with our kids in their pajamas. Sometimes we drive our kids to school wearing our pajamas. We know what's important, and we don't sweat the little details. I became an *experienced parent* one afternoon in a Barnes and Noble bathroom—there was no going back.

My Badass Minivan

Speaking of *no going back*—we eventually bought a minivan. When you buy a minivan, you are saying, "I have more than two kids, and I don't give a shit what people think of me anymore." The great thing about minivans is that there are so many of them. It isn't like buying a motorcycle with a sidecar or something—it's just a minivan. Minivans are a rite of passage for many parents, and to a certain degree, they are braggable. Like a scar or a bad haircut, minivans are supposed to be celebrated instead of hidden.

My minivan is awesome. It is literally falling apart. The doors make some kind of weird machine gun sound when they lock. The VCR stopped working, the engine light comes on intermittently, and it always says we need an oil change. We maintain our minivan about as regularly as you can: new tires, tune-ups, oil changes, alignments, etc. It doesn't seem to matter though. Our A/C system had to be replaced, almost all of our automatic locks have failed, and even our windows have been sticking lately. With less than 100K miles of wear and tear, I can only point to one culprit—children.

The exact reason that necessitates having a minivan in the first place is the same reason why they fall apart so fast. Besides the normal marks and dents that kids make on everything you own, a minivan is assaulted on a totally different level.

The messes are so profound and complete in our minivan that it is difficult to find the strength to clean it. There are fast-food toys, napkins, hair clips, coloring books, clothing, and even money strewn throughout the interior. You know it is really bad when you see a perfectly good dollar on the ground, and you can't find the motivation to pick it up. Of course, I clean it inside and out every couple months, but it is still a minivan at the end of the day. And no matter how dilapidated, sticky, and stinky it is on the inside—it's still awesome.

Why My Minivan Is Awesome

My minivan is many things. First, and most importantly, it's a **chick magnet**. I am always surrounded by females when I'm in my minivan. Granted, those females are my daughters and my wife, but I still feel like a *rock star*. When I am riding in my minivan I *always* wear my $10 Target sunglasses, I always listen to the music (Kidz Bop), and I am always playing the drums on my steering wheel. Sometimes I think it would be cool to have a convertible minivan just so I could prove to everyone just how awesome I am. Alas, my awesomeness remains a well-kept secret.

My minivan is a taxi. I collect no fares and I get no tips, but I am always shuttling customers to and fro. My customers are Bella, Mady, and Sophia. They love being driven around in the minivan. It's like showing up to dance practice in a limo or a Lamborghini except the inside is cluttered, smells like week-old french fries, and has three safety kids' car seats.

My minivan rules because of some hot customizations. I have transformed the center change compartment into a hair clip holder. I have turned the floor into a humungous trash can. I have my own portable *boom box*—it's true. I've hooked my iPod into the radio via a transceiver, and it works almost 25 percent of the time. I have intelligently converted the girls' car seats into portable composting units. Want some nutrient-rich soil for your garden? Give me some fast food and a couple weeks to allow the burger meat and pressed chicken to break down completely.

My minivan rules most of all because of the memories. There are good times and bad times. There are times when we laughed together and times when we cried. There are even times when I almost ran off the road.

The Warning Swerve

On one fateful trip returning home from a vacation in Cape May, New Jersey, our family had an abnormally hellish ride home. Let me start by saying our daughters love seashells. Like all our trips to Cape May, the girls had collected dozens of respectable specimens and packed many of them to bring home. The girls even found conch shells. They ranged in size from about a half an inch in height to several inches. One of the most large and brilliant shells actually had a critter still inside and this resident, of course, did not want to come out. The only way to get the creature out of the shell was to cook him out. After boiling the shell with the mollusk inside for nearly ten minutes, the mollusk finally gave up the fight and let go of the shell.

The removal of this mollusk from the conch shell was the last thing we did before we packed our car and left for home. We noticed that the process had left the kitchen smelling offensive to say the least. We thought nothing of the stench in the kitchen since the creator of the smell was now gone and out of our lives . . . or so we thought.

At about the twenty-mile mark on our way home, our minivan began to smell like the **ocean's rear end**. The smell that envelops a family during long road trips is often unpleasant. However, this smell was different, and like a thick blanket of fog, it invaded the interior of our car. As the driver of the *stink-mobile*, I was beginning to get irritated—no check that, extremely upset with each passing stink-filled moment. To make matters worse, my kids (who desperately required the conch in the first place) were complaining.

"Ew! What is that smell?!" They were thrashing around like there was a bee in the car.

The sound of a child whining is probably the best form of birth control. When a mom and dad have had a tough day with the kids, usually the last thing on their minds is, "You know what? Let's have another." I think a few well-placed, whiny kids could change the teenage pregnancy statistics in the United States overnight. My particular children were covering their noses and asking for the smell to go away. I know my kids think highly of me, but besides lighting the vehicle on fire (which I was thinking of doing), there was little I could do to mask the offensive scent that surrounded us. I was starting to wonder if the smell would ever come out of the car. I mean, how many pine-scented car fresheners would it take to diffuse the smell of rotting mollusk?

Like all parents, I have a breaking point. Apparently, my breaking point requires the following ingredients: horrific odor, whiny kids, long car ride, and sand in my shorts. Up to this point, my wife, bless her soul, had been trying to stifle the whining coming from the backseats of our minivan; it was now my turn. I had had enough.

As I turned to tell my progeny to remain silent for the rest of their natural-born lives, the car did a small swerve. Like when Reese married peanut butter and chocolate, I discovered something groundbreaking with that *swerve*. It turns out that the *swerve* was a more effective disciplinary measure than anything I could ever say out loud to my kids. The *swerve* wasn't dangerous or damaging in any way. It was just enough of a wild maneuver to give my daughters pause. The *swerve*, coupled with the mad look in my eyes, transformed my whiny, obnoxious girls into silent, compliant angels. I am not suggesting that you start swerving back and forth to get your children's attention, but it rescued me once.

Memoirs of a Minivan

The memories in our minivan started out five years ago with a long road trip to Niagara Falls, Canada. From that trip forward, the gray metallic vehicle has been the hub for many special moments in our family's life. Like the time when we couldn't figure out where a horrible smell was coming from for a few weeks, and then we finally found this treelike thing growing out of a strawberry milk shake spill.

I remember when we packed into the minivan to take Jodi to the hospital to deliver Sophia and the subsequent car ride home. I remember the way that the girls looked when they were smaller. I remember their transition from infant seats to toddler seats to the big-kid booster seats. I remember them watching *Parent Trap* around a thousand times until I was able to memorize all the words of each scene. It's the good and bad times that we've shared together that make my minivan a thing of beauty. Even that car ride home from Cape May, New Jersey, when a rotting mollusk almost made me crash us is a piece of that awesome puzzle. The minivan is a metaphor for our family, and my family is nothing to be ashamed of.

Creating Mini-Mes: Benefits of Being a Stay-at-Home Dad

I personally think it is more challenging staying home with kids than it is to work. Your days consist of diapers, bottles, smells, messes—all the stuff I already covered, but there are some amazing perks.

Milestones

Being a full-time dad is a major challenge, but there are some major rewards. Being a dad is a lot like coaching; you suffer through the bad and revel in the good. As a full-time dad, you will be there when your kid starts to roll and crawl for the first time. You will watch them as they start cruising around and, eventually, walking on their own. As your child mutters their first sounds—you will hear them. The milestones are sometimes concrete and universally acknowledged, but oftentimes, they are a bit more subtle.

For instance, when my kid graduated out of formula or breast milk was always great for me as a stay-at-home dad. I didn't have all the bottle preparation anymore—things just got easier. Another graduation that goes unnoticed is the "I can feed myself" milestone. There are so many of these moments that all point to a child becoming someone who is more independent and self-sufficient that receive little to no press. One of my favorite graduations or milestones is when a child understands and demonstrates proficiency in buckling themselves into their car seats.

Like a coach, you are teaching your child the whole way through all these moments in their lives, offering encouragement and praise. Their accomplishments speak to you as a parent just as much as they speak to your child as a growing, learning individual. It is hard to not be proud as you see your kids navigate the challenging world around them.

Manners

As the full-time parent, you are the full-time influencer of your children. What they do reflects on you and the example you are setting for them at home. Another opportunity for stay-at-home parents is to coach your children to use manners.

Something that always makes me feel good is to see my girls use their manners appropriately. I think children should respect adults, and adults should respect children. It all begins with the simple lesson of teaching your children "please" and "thank-you." I think we all have seen some of those obnoxious kids that think they are entitled to every cookie, candy, and chewy snack within a five-mile radius. It is ugly to see a kid that has no manners, and I think it warms everyone's heart to see a child who has been taught respect. I can safely say my kids have been guilty of being both the obnoxious kid and the respectful one, but thankfully, they generally reside in the latter.

Love

Dads should coach love. As a stay-at-home dad to three daughters, I feel my responsibility is huge. I need to make sure that they see what a proper husband and dad should be through the example I set.

Two women have impacted me greatly as a dad. They were both relative strangers. One was a classmate at Towson University. This was shortly after the time we had Isabella. The whole class knew, but she took a greater interest in the announcement. I remember on the last day of class she told me, "You take care of your daughter—love her." It was a simple bit of advice, but the look in the woman's eyes was so sincere that it has stayed with me to this day.

The other woman I met during an everyday shopping trip. She noticed I had a daughter and started talking to me about her father and how she had a lot of sisters. She told me, "The most important person in a daughter's life is their father." That advice always struck me as profoundly true.

By being a loving, respectful husband, my daughters are learning what is acceptable behavior by the way I treat my wife. I tell my girls all the time how much I love them, and they have learned to respond in kind. I think many little girls are supersweet by nature, but I would like to take some of the credit for how loving our girls are.

It is a huge source of pride for me when my girls talk about how they love their friends and family members. You can throw all the other junk out, but I can be assured I am doing a good job when my girls tell me they love me—all the time.

Mini-Mes

As a stay-at-home dad, my girls learn culture, morality, and when to goof around through the example I set every day. For instance, I quote movie lines all the time. One of my favorite lines that I use with my kids is from the movie *Aliens*. I think I have said, "Move like you got a purpose, people," about a thousand times. For some odd reason, I am proud when I hear them copy me and use my lines with each other or with me.

Besides passing down one-liners, I also love to make people laugh, and this sense of humor is something I can safely say I have handed down to my girls. Lastly, my father taught me through example how important humility is—and whether it is in sports, academics, or their personal lives—I strive to teach my girls the lesson of humility. It is so cool to see my girls miss an opportunity to brag simply because it isn't part of their culture at home.

As your kids grow up from infants to toddlers to kids in school, you can see your influence in how they act. The litmus test for my body of work is how my children behave. Are they well adjusted? Are they happy? Are they respectful and humble? Are they confident? Are they well behaved in public settings? I take pride in my kids as a stay-at-home dad because they are my full-time occupation. When strangers, friends, and family members compliment my kids—they are complimenting me.

Naps

Naps are probably the most awesome thing that God invented. If I could choose between naps and gold, I would pick naps. Naps happen when you are a stay-at-home parent—period. Naps don't happen when you are working a day job (well, at least they aren't supposed to). Some days, when I am stressed-out from my inability to find a child's missing shoe or if the dishes are getting me down, I just look over at my friend **Mr. Comfy Green Couch** and nod in affirmation.

I have become a nap connoisseur in my nine-plus-year stint as a stay-at-home dad, and I have done it all. I have done the *mid-morning-I-went-to-bed-late-last-night nap*, I have done the *I-just-ate-too-much-in-the-middle-of-the-day-thank-goodness-my-toddler-wants-to-relax-too nap*, and the *I-can't-believe-I-folded-six-loads-of-laundry-and-mowed-the-lawn-and-it-is-only-eleven-in-the-morning nap*. To take a nap, you will need your child to be asleep as well—no sleeping on the job; you will need a comfy spot to sleep, and you will need to be tired. Also, I have found that toddlers make great nap partners.

Food

When you are home, you can literally eat yourself into oblivion. Food is all around you, and there is nothing stopping you from eating it. I have become a much better baker since I became a stay-at-home dad. Homemade breads, cakes, brownies, biscuits—you name it; I have baked it. Cooking is fun too. I have enjoyed experimenting with new recipes and adding my spin on old ones. For instance, I love spicy food, so instead of just plain old broccoli and cheese soup, I like to make broccoli and smoked Gouda soup with ancho chilies. Anyone will tell you my mashed potatoes are the bomb, and if you don't think my buffalo wings are some of the best you have ever tasted—you have issues.

With all this access to food, it can be overwhelming; but most people would say that two of their favorite things in the world are sleeping and eating, and both are available if you play your cards right.

Being a Kid Again

I love cartoons. I love toys. Kids love both of these things. Now that I am around kids all the time, I can watch cartoons and play with toys—sometimes I can do both at the same time. There is nothing like building a Lego castle while watching the *Misadventures of Flapjack* or *Spongebob Squarepants*. Stay-at-home parents have an excuse as to why they are watching shows like *Phineas and Ferb* or *The Mighty B!* No one questions them; no one tells them to "grow up." It is just part of the job.

When you stay home with the kids, you can goof off and play with the kids *like a kid*. A lot of the moms at the outdoor parks are either passive observers or very cautious followers, kind of like a kiddy-secret service, making sure their kids don't mangle themselves. Not me, I like being a part of the action. I mean, I am not ruining a game of tag, but I do enjoy climbing, going down the occasional slide with them, and playing Wiffleball or Frisbee when we hit the park scene. Also, acting like a kid, I have found, really reduces your stress level; and I highly recommend it to all stay-at-home parents.

TV

Like I mentioned before, cartoons are great, and I get my fair share; but there are other awesome shows on TV. *Sportscenter* is one such show that is always available. You can do the dishes with Kenny Mayne in the background or fold laundry while you watch the highlights from last night's action. During the Men's NCAA Basketball Tournament, you can watch the opening games from the comfort of your home while other folks are scrambling around the office Internet trying to get updates.

Bottom-line, the TV can be on when you want it on—although, many times it will need to be on a kid's channel.

Personal Hygiene

If you don't want to shave—don't do it. If you think the clothes you wore for the last two days still have life—keep wearing them. It is your show. You can shower biweekly and wear baseball hats 24/7 if you like. I don't condone this kind of behavior though as it will result in a steep drop off in your sex life and perhaps acne, the common cold, and other health concerns. Bottom-line, if you want to take a day off from maintaining yourself—feel free.

It's Your Show

You are the boss of your house. If you want to play music all day and do housework in your boxer shorts, that's your prerogative. The typical day job has set ideas of what is allowable behavior during work hours—not so much for the stay-at-home crowd. Using the vacuum as a pretend microphone or making loud monster roars when you are chasing your kids around won't get you fired. Being a goofy, active parent is actually a good thing, and kids totally gravitate toward it.

Want to play Xbox while you do the laundry? Who's stopping you? Moms have scrapbooking and *Oprah*; dads should be allowed to pursue their hobbies and interests while they are at home too. If you like mountain biking, get a trailer ASAP and start riding everywhere you go. Your kids will love it, and the exercise and vitamin D will benefit you. You're the boss each and every day—take advantage of it.

Summing It Up

Being a full-time parent has become a source of pride for me. As a stay-at-home dad, you are there when they take their first steps to when they get on the bus for the first time. You are both a coach and a caregiver. Your influence helps your children overcome gender limitations and see a world without barriers. We give our kids the best parts of us and mold them with humor, patience, and respect. We are an influence that continues to be felt with each passing day, month, and year. The next time someone asks you what you do for a living don't be bashful. Tell them you are making the world a better place one day at a time.

The Stay-at-Home Dad
Goes Back to Work

I remember going through an identity crisis around the time we had the miscarriage. I was mentally prepared to be a stay-at-home parent for another five years. I was stopped in my tracks. I had to start thinking about reentering the workforce. *What was I going to do? What did I have to offer? What type of job should I get?* Sophia was only a couple years away from going to elementary school. I needed to start thinking about a career that would be flexible. I needed to find a job that would let me be there when the kids got off the bus. It had to be something that could bring in some money. It had to be something worth taking seriously. I was anxious just thinking about my prospects.

Enter Deb Zavoyna. I remember confiding in my playgroup friends about my thoughts about work and going back to work. I told them that I was worried that I couldn't find something flexible enough to fit our family's needs and something that I would enjoy. I remember Deb asking, "Well, Joe, what do you like to do? What would you do if you could choose your perfect job?"

I thought about it for a minute and said, "I always said that I would love to write for a living."

"Well, have you ever thought about blogging?" she asked.

"Blogging? No, I haven't," I replied.

"I think it would be perfect for you. You could write about being a stay-at-home dad. I am sure there are a lot of people interested in what your days are like," she said. "If you enjoy it and get noticed, then maybe writing is for you. Maybe you could make a career out of it."

"You know what, that's a great idea." She hit the nail on the head. I could practice writing through a blog and just see where it led. If it turned out it was meant to be, then it would be an ideal job. It would easily be flexible enough to fit around any schedule. It could bring in some extra money, and there's no telling where Internet ventures can lead. So I dove into the world of blogging. I started Joeprah.com.

Joeprah was a play on words. Think *Oprah* with *Joe* in the front. I did just what Deb told me to do. I wrote about being a stay-at-home dad. Blogging gave me direction when I needed it most. Soon after I started blogging, I was noticed. Articles I wrote were mentioned in *Newsweek, LA Times,* and Yahoo!. I thought my articles or posts were basically sophomoric humor, but apparently, they spoke to people.

After a year or so of blogging, I was offered a paid gig writing for *The Examiner* as the *National Fatherhood Examiner*. Little by little, I made money, but more than that, I could see that I could take writing seriously once the girls were in school.

Thinking about my inevitable return to work has always given me a certain amount of anxiety. The expectations for stay-at-home dads are different than they are for stay-at-home moms. If a stay-at-home mom continues to stay home after the kids are in school, our society says, "That's fine." Stay-at-home dads, however, are *expected* to return to work. *Why? Why aren't moms expected to go back to work? What does this mean for my three daughters?*

Raising three daughters over the last nine years has taught me that our society has a vision of what it wants our little girls to grow up to be. My girls have been bombarded with advertisements and images of pink princesses. They see their friends playing with glamorous, anorexic, borderline, slutty dolls. There are even tight-fitting toddler outfits for sale at the stores. TV shows encourage girls to be popular, have lots of money, and be ditzy. The expectations are troublesome to say the least.

I think these expectations carry over into adulthood, making it harder for women to pursue their careers than it should be. They are told that they can serve their families best by staying home with the kids. It isn't fair to women, and stay-at-home moms have been rebelling. They are starting their own businesses, becoming inventors, and creating opportunities where none existed. They are redefining themselves. But stay-at-home moms' egos aren't just wrapped up in what they contribute via dollars and cents. Most moms understand the importance and value in taking care of a family, and they do what is best for the family.

What about men?

Men have a tough time separating ego and money, and it limits us. Our expectations have led us to associate success in our careers as the ultimate gauge of our value to our families. We seem to envy the guy with the bigger house instead of the guy with the happiest family.

With women valued less in the workforce and men not being respected at home, where is the middle ground?

With an influx of dads raising their families *full-time,* there is slowly a shift in our society's attitudes. Each dad who has that unique opportunity to watch his kids grow up is not only making a difference to his family, but also to the society we live in. Each stay-at-home dad is teaching his sons and daughters an important lesson about equality. We are teaching our kids that it's OK for men to scrub toilets. We are saying it's OK for women to provide for a family. We are breaking down barriers.

So as I close the chapter on my stay-at-home-dad days, my main concern isn't what I will add to our pocketbook, but what I have done to prepare my girls for the world.

Index

L

LAC (Late by Association Club), 152–53
lactation consultant, 46
LA Times, 168
learned helplessness, 5, 39–40
Leatherman, 67
Lego, 164
Lifetime Channel, 91

M

Madison (neighborhood baby), 70–71
Mady. *See* Schatz, Madeleine
"Mary Had a Little Lamb," 74
Mayne, Kenny, 165
McDonalds, 154
Men's NCAA Basketball Tournament, 165
Mighty B! The, 164
minivan, 156–60
Misadventures of Flapjack, The, 164
M&M's, 125
moms
  stay-at-home, 10, 17–18, 66, 76, 80, 168
  thought of as better parents, 40
Monsters, Inc., 115
Mozart, 61
Murray, Bill, 66

N

National Fatherhood Examiner, 168
Newsweek, 168
NFL (National Football League), 41, 77

Niagara Falls, Canada, 159

O

1-2-3 Magic: Effective Discipline for Children 2-12 (Phelan), 106
OPK (other people's kids), 117–19
Oprah, 21, 76, 166, 168

P

Pack n Plays, 64
parenting pick, 137
parenting sleight of hand, 104
parents
  categories, 119
  types of
    experienced, 156
    first-time, 61
    stay-at-home, 49, 62, 66, 69, 162–65, 167
Parent Trap, 160
Partnership Parenting (Pruett), 42
Patty (neighbor), 71
Phelan, Thomas
  1-2-3 Magic: Effective Discipline for Children 2-12, 106
Phineas and Ferb, 164
playgroup, 31, 76, 85, 167
  Bagel Club, 18, 20–21, 77, 80
  conversations, 77–79
  dads-only, 80
  hosting a, 79
  moms' terms and phrases, 78
  sharing, 81–84
    bait and switch, 82–83
    go fetch, 83
Polar Express, 110

characteristics, 27, 29
conversation about money, 145
destruction issues, 135
at home with Mom, 139–40
Sharpie incident, 86–87
toddler logic, 101
sex (after kids), 120
fatigue, 121
infants and babies hating sex, 121
things to avoid (for the husband), 124–26
things to do (for the wife), 127–29
tips, 122–24
special day philosophy, 29
Spongebob Squarepants, 164
Sportscenter, 76, 165
Steve (neighbor), 22
Swiss Army knife, 67

T

Target, 154, 157
Teddy Grahams, 67, 79
thuds, kinds of, 86
Titanic, 154
toddler
  definition, 95
  discipline, 106
    explanation, 103
    1-2-3 Magic, 106
    parenting sleight of hand, 104
    time-out, 106–7
  fashion, 96
  gifts, 99
  how they get around, 97–99
  language, 99
  logic, 100, 102
  me-ists, 84
  offering choices, 105–6

public places and, 107
  movies, 109–10
  restaurants, 108
shoe dyslexic, 95
tendency to grab, 92–93
top-off status, 143
wanting to get out of the crib, 93
Towson, Maryland, 13
Towson University, 162
Toys "R" Us, 154
Tramontana, Courtney, 31, 77–78
Transformers, 17, 40
"Twinkle, Twinkle Little Star," 74
Tylenol, 107

W

Water World, 50
Wazowski, Mike, 115
"Wheels on the Bus," 74
Wiffleball, 149–50, 165

X

Xbox, 166

Y

Yahoo! 168
Yale Child Studies Center, 42
YMCA, 73

Z

Zavoyna, Deb, 31, 77–78, 167–68

22755991R00094

Made in the USA
Lexington, KY
12 May 2013